Enjoy Your Solo

How to Be Great at Being Single

Mary Delia Allen

Enjoy Your Solo

ISBN: 979-8-9852258-0-8

Mary Delia Allen

enjoyyoursolobook@gmail.com

www.themarydelia.com

KAYWOOD
PRESS

Contents

Introduction.. 1

Who Am I?... 7

A Special Note.. 15

Chapter One Great Singles to Admire 17

Chapter Two The Upsides of the Downsides of Being Single 23

Chapter Three Searching for Love................................. 31

Chapter Four Really Be Single 37

Chapter Five Sex in the Solo.. 43

Chapter Six Heal Grief 51

Chapter Seven Closing Up Shop 59

Chapter Eight Choose Your Thoughts............................ 63

Chapter Nine Solo Life Vs. Partner Life 69

Chapter Ten Know Yourself to Be Selfless 75

Chapter Eleven Feeling Lonely Use T.R.A.P.S. and S.P.A.R.K. Yourself .. 81

Chapter Twelve Rituals and Routines 89

Chapter Thirteen Friends and Socializing....................... 95

Chapter Fourteen The Cocktail Party Question................. 103

Chapter Fifteen Allies 109

Chapter Sixteen Get an Idiot Mirror 117

Chapter Seventeen Beware the Friendly Distractions.......... 123

Chapter Eighteen Party for One: Staying In................... 131

Chapter Nineteen Party of One: Going Out Solo 137

Chapter Twenty Party Beyond One: Going Out to Connect.... 151

Chapter Twenty-One The Future: Don't Wait 159

Chapter Twenty-Two Money: It's All Yours.. 167

Chapter Twenty-Three Side Hustles 173

Chapter Twenty-Four The End of Life.. 179

Chapter Twenty-Five Live Well and Have Standards............................... 185

Final Note 193

Call to Action.. 195

Acknowledgements.. 197

Introduction

You are the star of your own life and it's already happening, with or without someone playing a lead opposite you. Time without a partner can be your time to shine. Solos don't last forever, but if you do them right, they can be a highlight on life's journey.

Picture a concert with a soloist. One instrument or voice is given a celebrated spotlight. When it comes time for the solo – all the other instruments and all the other performers are quiet. The audience focuses entirely on the person performing the solo. The soloist is dedicated fully to their own performance. The audience is hushed and excited, waiting for the performance. The solo is a highlighted part of the show. With a fresh approach, that's how being single can be. Just like a music solo, you will have to create, prepare, and enter the spotlight alone. Only you can make this time in your life sing.

There are different paths to the solo life.

Maybe you are newly single and happy about it. Single and ready to mingle! Either way, this is a wonderful manual for setting up your alone time with lots of advice on enjoying your own company and making yourself happy first, which is the very best foundation to starting your solo journey.

On the other extreme, maybe you are shocked and surprised and have been slammed into being single through abandonment or the passing of a partner. This is a look at *all* facets of singlehood and a good starter course if you've been in a longtime partnership. You'll find advice and proactive strategies for managing your time and interactions to find fulfillment on this new path.

Perhaps your last partnership ended poorly. You are hurt or angry or feeling rejected. You think about your ex—why things ended or how things were *supposed* to turn out. You can stay in those feelings of anger and hurt, or you can work to see this change as a gift of a new life you can give yourself. There are insights here on accepting your solo status and taking steps to create a new post-relationship life where you give yourself the life you want.

Maybe you haven't had a close love relationship and you just feel like a single on simmer. You've dated but haven't had much choice in ending up single. Making your life the best solo it can be, will bring you more contentment and perspective in this season of your life.

Lastly, maybe you are very content being single, thank you very much. You've been the center of your life for a long time. You feel stable and comfortable. Or you've been single for a short time, but you feel comfortable with the choice to be single.

Regardless of how you arrived, this book is about YOU. As the boss of your life, where you put your energy and focus is all up to you. Life at any stage is a gift, so commit to viewing this solo season as one where you can be your best! Create a solo you love right now.

Is there something in your life you think you should "fix" or change for a partner? Are you waiting to be with a partner before improving your life? Do you think of getting into a relationship as a kind of graduation? You think, *I'll work on my finances, my health, taking on more responsibilities, quitting bad habits, improving my life when it's more than just me.* Why are YOU not enough to make those changes? What are you waiting for? Why would you make more effort for a partner than you would for YOURSELF?

While the perfect partner could show up tomorrow, maybe your solo will last a long time. Or a lifetime. Maybe the perfect partner is a few years away. Make this solo time count. Living your best life without a romantic partner can be very rewarding. When/If the great partner shows up for you, do you want to say, "Wait! I'm going start to get it together," or, "I'm having a wonderful time; hop in, let's have a wonderful time together!"?

Another thing about partners is they will come and go. While your relationship with yourself is forever, a solo is wonderful to get to know yourself without distraction.

Speaking of relationships, being in one is work. To have a successful partnership, you need to put in time and effort. Being a good partner requires being thoughtful in your interactions, creating rituals, and making your relationship a priority for it to be worthwhile and grow. Those same concepts equally apply to single life. Positive outcomes require thought and effort. The good news is when you are single, the work you are doing is on yourself, so your subject is always available and hopefully enthused!

You get to choose what you want to do with your solo. Is your idea of the perfect weekend spent prepping for a marathon, reading a novel in two days, or taking a weekend trip with friends—old or new? In the solo, the choice is yours.

Your energy can be redirected to yourself in a healthy way to benefit you. It requires thoughtful action to appreciate your solo status through the values you choose, how you spend your time, and how you approach your life.

I've mentioned relationships so many times already because relationships have been the culturally accepted norm for so long. Throughout most of history, marriage was a political and monetary arrangement. Today, the pressure to marry the prince next door to increase your family's land holdings, snag a spouse to ensure a financial future, or couple up to survive the next winter isn't as common. Society has more people single for longer and at different stages of life than ever before.

Despite all the messages (familial, practical, religious, marketing, your own life goals) that propel you toward being coupled, it is almost *expected* that you will be without a romantic partner during various stages of your life. People are getting married later in life. Marriages and relationships change or end. Enjoy this single stage and allow for your own growth and happiness. This time in your life without a partner is a gift that only you can give yourself.

Now that we've discussed what a solo is, let's talk about what this book is not. If you picked up this book to learn about how to find a partner, be better at dating, or attract a partner, then you've come to the wrong place. This book is about YOU and your solo. There are a million books on dating, coupling, and romance...go find one of those. Searching for love and wanting a partner is valid, but that can't be done twenty-four hours a day. Actively planning and providing your own happiness through positive thoughts and actions? That can be done all day long, every day.

Enjoy Your Solo offers a way to look at all parts of being single. Some may apply to you, others may not. Maybe you're ready to hear and examine parts of your solo life, maybe you won't be ready until a year from now. The goal is to not rush through this solo and run toward the next partner or stay living in the past when you had a partner. Instead, you can—to borrow a phrase—lean in to your own solo.

You can choose to make yourself the star of your show.

Who Am I?

I love men. I love romantic love and relationships. I love engagement rings and wedding days. I respect commitment, families, and long-standing relationships—married, common law, gay or straight. I believe those are wonderful, cherished parts of life. I do not believe they are the *only* parts of life despite what romantic comedies, marketing, and tradition might promote.

I have been single forever. Statistically, shockingly single forever.

Of course, you want to know *why* I have been single for so long. Because I am good at it and I never got a better offer. I created a wonderful life built to fit me well. I found plenty to do and fun to have while looking for a partner I never found. In *Enjoy Your Solo*, I'm going share my perspective on why being single is fantastic, the tools for self-reflection, and actionable steps to start seriously enjoying your solo right now.

We are in a new era of what being single looks and feels like. My intention with this book is to change how the solo is viewed and, more importantly, experienced! I admire those who forge a new life after the loss of a partnership. I celebrate people making the most of their time before or between romantic partnerships. I am rooting for all those fighting their way back to making the most of their life after all kinds of romantic disappointments.

The Bachelor, 90 Day Fiancé, and *Say Yes to the Dress*

are so popular and celebrate finding The One. I truly wish there were shows like *Divorce Rehab*, *Getting Your Life Back*, *Solo Vacation Adventures*, and *365 Days of Living Alone for the First Time*. These would follow the trials and triumphs of something besides pursuing romance. Heck, how about popular culture celebrating something beyond finding a partner with beautiful backdrops and exciting cliffhangers on a show like *Say Yes to the Scrubs — Research Doctors Promote Their Groundbreaking Study Findings*. Maybe giving cancer-curing doctors this kind of attention is not entertainment, but I like what it would say about our values.

I guess *Grey's Anatomy* celebrates doctors saving lives, but there sure is a lot of McSteamy and McDreamy and bed-hopping love pursuits on that show. That's television, not real life. In fact, the show's creator, Shonda Rhimes, has a whole chapter on happily committing to never getting married herself in her wonderful book *A Year of Yes*. Read that book. Shonda is a lady who is making a solo look amazing.

I want to say I'm a singles expert, but that's like saying I'm a human expert. Being single is like being human—it's individual for all of us. Everyone arrives at being single for different reasons, lengths of time, and attitudes. And we all have to define what "being great" is for ourselves. But I do have personal and work experience that gives me insight into all types of single journeys.

Part of my motivation to write *Enjoy Your Solo* was my decade as a professional tour guide, escorting singles on vacation. I traveled with all kinds of people who were single for all sorts of reasons and often at different stages of singlehood with many different motivations for joining a vacation just for people who are single. As a social hostess, my goal was to transform a group that had just met into friends. As a group leader, I was also a protector. Since my guests traveled alone, I was to be available to assist if they were injured, fell ill, got bad news from home, or needed social advice or a pep talk. I learned a lot about singles' struggles and solutions. I also saw a lot of singles have a ton of fun. This experience showed me being solo is a valid and wonderful time of life!

I've also had an exciting and fulfilling career in

event logistics that gives me a crazy travel schedule, a big circle of work friends, and positions that strictly forbid romance with clients. As a corporate meeting staffer, I learned to rebuff the come-ons of the traveling businessman. My job was to make sure the clients got on the bus to the airport after the meeting, not to sneak to his hotel room and hear about how his wife doesn't understand him. While leading singles vacations, I was there as an employee, not to canoodle with any of the single attendees. More importantly, the participants were there to socialize with one another, and taking the attention of the male participants would have been unfair to the group I was leading and probably hit me in the pocketbook come gratuity time at the end of the vacation.

Altogether, I got in the habit of dodging romantic attention. Add to that a pretty independent spirit and I created an awesome single life.

I never wrote "Mr. and Mrs. So-and-So" on my notebook in school. I never dreamed of my monogram with his monogram, which became *our* monogram. I never imagined a long list of attributes of a partner down to a specific look we would have together as a couple. I never envisioned a family life, naming the children and deciding what color the kitchen would be in my coupled-up fantasies. I was less attached to a traditional path and more open to a life on my own.

Sure, I've had crushes and carried torches. I've had men fall for me. I've had entanglements I could talk endlessly about at the time, and now, in hindsight, can barely explain or honestly recall. I've heard the words "I love you." I've said them less. If I am honest, there were men who could have been the Mr. to my Mrs., but it never truly called to me. I had sexless boyfriends and a few only for sex partners. My experience as one half of a couple has been limited. I've never received a wedding invitation and thought, *I'll take Mr. Wonderful as my date.* I have really been solo in this world. I've done it for a couple decades, and I've learned to do it really well.

I've never had sex on my birthday. I am THAT single well into my forties. I've flipped the TV channel when the jewelry commercials come on to avoid thinking of the proposals and gifts I have not received. I've had to remind myself at a few baby and bridal showers that life brings the right situations to you at the right time. I've been on girls' vacations only to figure out that I had outgrown certain antics. I've run my own financials and decorated my own homes. By always trying to make the most of every experience, anyone can master this single life! Like many others, I hope for another phase with a partner, but until then, I want to share my solo building strategies so that you can see your own solo in a positive new light.

There's an old joke about a man being stuck in a hole and another man comes along. The man stuck in the hole says, "Hey, I'm stuck and need help," and the second man jumps in the hole. The first man says, "Why did you do that? Now we're both stuck!" The second man replies, "Yes, but I've been here before, and I know the way out."

If you feel you are in a deep hole or even just a shallow rut of solo life, I've been there, and I know the way out.

A Special Note

To Single Parents

You can do it! Obviously, parenting is the most important job, but putting effort and thought into building your own solo life will make you a happier single parent and provide you with the tools to continue to make yourself happy as your children grow.

To Gentleman and The Non-Straight

I am a heterosexual woman of a certain (starting to be middle) age. The advice is based on my experience, so it's a lady-heavy perspective, but I firmly believe the concepts of seizing your opportunity to be the very best solo through self-examination and positive action are universal. I hope you'll forgive my female pronouns and viewpoint and know that I am rooting for *all* parties seeking to live their best in the time spent without a romantic partner.

Since The Pandemic

The whole world has had a hands-on lesson in enjoying isolation. TikTok dances, sweatpants, screens, and solo time were all on the rise, but so were new ways of staying in touch, enjoying hobbies, and appreciating our social lives. The pandemic has forever changed how we work, live, and socialize. The messages here on enjoying your own company and building a solo life that makes you happy no matter your circumstances has become all the more urgent in these changing times.

Chapter One

Great Singles to Admire

Life is not an ark; not everyone is paired up. Let's be aspirational and visit the idea of Great Singles — fictional and IRL (in real life).

Oprah

She never actually married Stedman. Although they have a committed partnership that looks pretty adorable on Instagram, Ms. Winfrey is single. She also has an amazing bestie relationship in Gayle. Their longtime bonded female friendship gets as much press as Stedman. Oprah also has billions of dollars, a TV network, a book club, and is making huge humanitarian impacts with her money and platform. She recommends books and they sell millions and change lives. All this while she grows vegetables, quotes Maya Angelo, and wears fashion athletic shoes and cool glasses. The news report does *not* read: "Still single Oprah Winfrey recommended a book today."

Jennifer Aniston

First, she's gorgeous. Google says she is worth $150 million. I say women of a certain age still pine for the Rachel haircut. *Friends* is part of the television lexicon. She married forever hunk and movie star Brad Pitt (five years), then later married and divorced hunkier in a different way Justin Theroux (two years). The media still portrays her as missing something since she is not a wife and mother. If you search online, you can find a 2011 *Good Morning America* interview where Aniston is asked about a breakup with the implied message: you are a sad single girl. And she replied, "My home wasn't destroyed in a natural disaster. My child didn't die in a war. Hearts mend." Amen.

All the Freaking Kardashians

Their children have fathers, and judging by appearances, they have sex with men on the regular. Just Kim and Khloe had televised wedding specials with lots of publicity when they were coupled, but mostly these ladies are unmarried. Lesson: even billions of dollars and followers doesn't make your marital status perfect.

Cher

Beautiful. Worth $305 million. Musical pop culture icon. Divorced Gregg Allman and Sonny Bono. Still single. Famously, her mother told her to find a rich man to marry and she replied, "Mom, a man is a luxury, not a necessity, and I am a rich man."

Princess Diana

Married a prince. Wonderful mother. Divorced only one year before her tragic passing, but I think she might have gone on to a wonderful single life. Some would argue even in her marriage she was living solo.

Betty White

She's making ninety-plus look amazing. Google her marital status. She's been married three times and single since 1981. In 2011, she told Anderson Cooper, "If I've had the best, who needs the rest?"

Vice President Kamala Harris

Vice President Kamala Harris didn't get married until her fifties.

Historically, there's Susan B. Anthony, Queen Elizabeth I, Clara Barton, and Jane Austen, among many. From the Wright Brothers to Jon Hamm, there are *plenty* of unmarried men.

And then there are the famous fictional singletons who made a very real impact.

Auntie Mame

Glamourous and rich, making everything a party and an adventure!

Mary Tyler Moore

Unmarried at the end of the TV series. She wasn't griping about living alone. Instead, she turned the world on with her smile. She had that cool apartment and a great job in the newsroom. Plus, she had Rhoda as the coolest single girl neighbor. That's a good-looking 1970s solo.

Bridget Jones

She did, in fact, sleep with Mark Darcy *and* Hugh Grant's character. She was chubby, a bit of a drunk, a sexpot, and 100 percent lovable. The biggest gift of the movie is a very accurate portrayal that some evenings are just couch, blankie, wine, and anthem singing…all by yourself. She's a good example of the push and pull between searching/being in/recovering from love while also wanting to chuck all the love business and keep a journal and love yourself just as you are.

The Sex in the City Gals

Points for portraying the solo stage of life and strong

friendships with great outfits topped with flawless hair. Demerits for so much time and energy spent on the pursuit of men without showing at least a bit of the grind it takes to get those wardrobes, homes, and handbags.

As you think of these famous soloists, is there anyone in *your* life you admire who stayed single? Maybe they spent their time and energy on a career. Or family. Or had adventures. Look around your own world for singles to admire.

Chapter Two

The Upsides of the Downsides
of Being Single

Being single is often seen as a temporary time or a throwaway period in your life.

Are you seeing anyone? Do you want to be married by the time you are thirty? You're getting divorced? Have you met anyone? You are making a life change – what if you meet someone? This quest to rush through being single and couple up is outdated. People are getting married later. Ending marriages more. Not getting married at all.

Let's abandon the idea that being single is a wasted time of life. A time one should rush through to find a partner. Being single is a cherished and valid season to learn about how to make yourself content on your own.

You are a Family of One. Complete.

You are not half of something or waiting to be something. You are more than enough. There is no graduation to coupledom. You might be single as a young person and single again after a long partnership. Both seasons by yourself are worthwhile times in your life. When we choose to see ourselves this way, the world will follow.

Being single allows all the parts of yourself to surface and blossom. What are your passions? What's your daily rhythm? What makes you excited? What helps you overcome negative feelings? Where do you want to spend your time? Your money? Your energy? What a delicious possibility to see what you'll become all on your own!

Romantic Love Is Valid (but not the only game in town!)

Being solo means being without a romantic partner. Romantic love and partnerships are important because they happen on a soul level. It makes sense that being without romantic love can be felt at a soul level. However, it is a mistake to allow that longing of your soul for a romantic love to grow into a big missing piece of life. It is a solo season. Reasons for becoming or staying single can be deep-rooted and painful, but I believe the act of *living* single does not have to be unhappy or empty feeling.

Sometimes it can feel like the only love that "counts" is romantic love that comes in pairs. Dreaming of romantic love and hoping for a life with a partner is wonderful, but life does not start with a wedding ring. Your life has already started. Make the most of it. Remind yourself that lots of pairs are loveless and sometimes both halves of pairs spend a lot of time showing their unlovable side. Don't compare the best parts of coupledom to the worst of singlehood. That is not fair, mostly to you. No stage in life is perfect or without challenges.

Here's the thing—being in a couple is wonderful, but it's pretty great to be solo too.

When the stakes are the most important positive feelings we have in life, like love and validation, emotions run high. But look around you. Love and validation are always available to you. Being a partner in a couple can be a joyful and wonderful part of anyone's life, but it's not the only game in town.

Love is being a good friend, neighbor, professional, community member, helper, sibling, thought leader. Intimacy isn't just in a romantic partnership. Intimacy happens all the time. Show up when someone is hurting and needy and be helpful. Show up when someone is crabby and selfish and be kind. Show up when something good happens for someone and genuinely be happy for them. Showing up and contributing is intimacy. Showing up can happen in person, via text, in prayers, in phone calls and any other kind of tech. It's also the fastest path to you feeling valid and having love in your life.

Romantic love gets all the good press but being a good person to the people on your life's path offers plenty of love.

Your time and energy are finite. You can spend the time you allotted to intimacy staying in or being sad/mad/frustrated about broken relationships and loves lost or pursuing/dreaming your next relationship OR you can choose to spend that time on yourself, making the very best of your solo. Your life has started, and time spent without a partner is worthwhile.

Life Can Feel Like an Ark

Solo in a two-by-two world is a real thing. Being single versus in a couple affects so many areas of life in a practical way. If you are sharing one life with two people, you have double the number of resources — time, money, energy — to tackle that one life built for two. If you are single, you have to do it all yourself. (Hint: another way to think of it is you *get* to do it all yourself.) No compromises. No one compensates, so you have to grow and cover all your life yourself. That's part of the solo season and can have lots of benefits, like knowing you can depend on yourself and enjoying building your life exactly as you want it to be.

Meanwhile, marketing makes it seem like everyone is in a couple. It's easier to sell once to two people! The growth of more single households is new, and I predict marketing will catch up. And one specific marketing trick? The six-BILLION-dollar wedding industry wants to keep couples registering at Target. I think Target and Pottery Barn and Walmart could be marketing to caregivers or good neighbors or any of the millions of other roles besides "new spouse" when it comes to registry programs. Stay tuned. The more solos are enjoyed, the more the marketers will follow.

Life Is Hard

I love many things about being single and I am here to PREACH about it. I want #enjoyyoursolo to become part of the lexicon! I want to bring validation to the time of life without a partner and celebrate individuals building their best solos. I truly believe that a solo season can be a very happy part of your life's journey.

I know how to fill my time and make myself happy. I can socialize alone and entertain myself. I've become confident in being the head of my own household of one.

But for the longest time I blamed regular life challenges on being single.

I blamed my marital status for negative events

instead of facing the hard stuff more directly. I don't like the big Christmas holidays and I blamed it on being single. Turns out I just don't like the pressure, hassle, and materialism of Christmas. I've learned to create my own happiness that time of year and it did not have one darned thing to do with a partner despite what every holiday movie would have me believe. I thought not having a partner limited growth. Turns out I still grew. I got smarter, mellowed, matured, progressed in my career, changed cities, tackled health issues, grew, and pruned my circle of friends, and came along life's path successfully *all by myself.*

I wish I had seen the solo as its own valid stage of the game and given less weight to the idea that a partner would solve my problems. I would have saved myself a lot of grief about being single and probably found better acceptance and solutions to the harder parts of life's path faster. Choosing to reframe your single marital status to positively fit into the landscape of your life's path is very powerful.

Chapter Three

Searching for Love

Did you sneakily flip to this chapter first, hoping to see the tips and tricks for finding a partner? Sorry. There is zero dating advice here. None. You'll have to find another book on dating. There are a lot of them! Good luck in your search!

A lot of time and energy can be misspent in the name of pursuing a partner on topics like:

- Am I attractive enough? If only I were richer/thinner/smarter/bigger/smaller!

- Does he like me? Did he text? What does the text mean? What should I text back? What do all of my friends think of this text? (Hint: if you really like each other, texting does not need editing.)

•Why are they together? Why did he pick her? Why are they getting married? Why do they have what I don't? (Hint: comparison has no win.)

•Maybe Taylor Swift is wrong, and he *will* ride a white horse! I will only date someone who [insert any litany of physical attributes or incredibly specific—and unrealistic—characteristics]. I won't settle until I meet someone who meets my three pages of criteria. (Hint: no partner is perfect. There are not that many men over 6 foot tall – be open.)

•Should I have married my last boyfriend? Does divorce blacklist me from love? What is my ex doing right now? Was I not enough in my marriage? (Hint: this is a blame game where only you suffer.)

You can spend your time—endlessly—on these kinds of thoughts. You can be wine-soaked, carb-fueled, and surrounded by the empathetic nods of your girlfriends until you twist yourself, physically or emotionally, into whatever partner-attracting pretzel this self-defeating quagmire of thoughts demands of you. Be realistic. The arrival of a mate will bring upgrades *and* adjustments. The goal is to make yourself happy, with or without a partner. Happiness is attractive.

What if you still want a partner? Of course, you can be open for a partner. Just don't make it a defining circumstance of your life. If you take to heart the advice here that speaks to you and truly commit and concentrate on doing single very well, you will be making yourself a wonderful partner. The more you invest in yourself and seek what types of activities and people you truly enjoy, the more you have to offer a partner. The better the life you create is, the better you will attract a quality partnership. The happier you are, the better choice you will make in committing to a partner.

You can turn your focus inward and choose to build a life that is all your own. Building a life you love with yourself will quiet all this insecure noise and leave you open to all kinds of better connections. Sounds like a great place to search for a partner.

While we're on the topic of partners, let's keep a few things in mind regarding the biggest searching for love gripes.

There are no potential partners out there.

If a genie in a bottle promised you a perfect life of exactly your own design, with all the health, safety, and riches you could want, *but* the only way to get that perfect life would be to find a partner — you would find someone. The nice side of this fantasy are the "details," like health and wealth, are a given. That's a nice package to sell to a potential partner. And in a perfect world of your creation, a partner's imperfections surely can't have that much impact. You would snap up a partner and make your way to paradise quickly!

There are no "good" potential partners.

If you were trapped on a desert island long enough with any person on earth, you would find a way to love that person. Time and circumstance would breed interdependence…that would lead to caring…which likely could lead to love. Anyone on earth. At some point they would stack some wood or hand you a leaf or make a funny joke about waves and you would be like, *OK, he's a good dude.*

There are no potential partners where I live.

Love is not going to run out. It's not sushi at a buffet or toilet paper in a pandemic. Google the census in your state or county and see how many single members of the opposite sex there are in your age category. It's a lot.

The partner search conundrum.

Do you have to go out and search high and low to find love? Or will love simply appear as promised in the movies? "It's a numbers game to find someone!" someone will say to you urgently. Then a moment later, someone will say, "Just stop looking and relax! That's how you find love," as if that's such an obvious path. I think both approaches can work depending on timing, your life goals, and the energy you want to commit. But does this question matter if you have built a solo life you love enough to have something wonderful to share no matter how or when a partner shows up?

Consider these concepts and let them bring you calm and the confidence to decide how to split your finite time and energy between pursuing a partner and building your solo. As you read on, you'll assess your single life and choose the steps you want to take to enjoy your solo more. Before you do that, stop and think what kind of role you want searching for love to take in your life. Maybe you want to take a break from dating, or you are putting a lot of energy into dating. Entirely up to you.

Just to sneak in one *tiny* bite of dating advice: the happier your solo life, the more resilient you feel dating.

Chapter Four

Really Be Single

It's all right to give yourself a dating and relationships hiatus. It's very much OK to focus on yourself. You are going to be 50 percent of your next relationship with a partner and 100 percent the person you are with for the rest of your life.

There is power in settling in and being single. You never know what you'll learn about yourself!

I went to Paris on a solo trip. When I booked it, I was online flirting with a guy from Denmark and had visions of Danish love in French Paris. The Dane declined to join and faded away. Admittedly, I planned the trip telling myself I was happy to go alone but was secretly wishing/hoping the Dane would come to his senses and join me. It's OK to sidestep your way into single adventures sometimes.

I had already visited Paris, so when I arrived, I found my interest in The City of Lights was a bit lackluster. At the time, I lived in Chicago and tried to approach the trip as "urban girl visits an urban place," not as a traditional tourist with a packed itinerary to catch all the sights. Instead, I gave myself a very easy schedule. No bounding out of bed to race through the Louvre or climb the Eiffel Tower. I did discover something very important about myself as a single on this international adventure. I hugely enjoyed French breads and cheeses and...I was *exhausted*. I was traveling a ton for work at the time. I was in my early thirties and always high energy up to that point. I had been able to get away with being both a morning person *and* a night person. But those days were ending.

I needed a true break. A hard reset.

I don't know if it was the soft Parisian light coming in the window or the perfect weight of the European duvet (which I can recall more intimately than the touch of past lovers), but I slept about twenty hours a day for four days. I crossed an ocean and took a snooze *a la*

Francaise. If this were a Lifetime movie, I would have met a handsome stranger for a fling while wearing cleverly tied scarves. Instead, the most interaction I recall was shooing away the maid.

No, you may not make this bed; I am sleeping in it.

Lesson learned. I needed to improve my sleep regimen. Plus, one can eat a great deal of carbs in four hours a day. *Merci.*

Not the expected lesson, but very valuable just the same!

Are you always imagining a future that will start when you find a perfect partner? Or do you often find yourself reminiscing about an ex? Are you attending activities you are only mildly interested in because "maybe you'll meet someone"? That's OK sometimes …but be motivated by what you really want to be doing. Do you go back in time to younger days when things were easier or better? Little mental visits to those times are fine. They can help us see what we want…or don't. But after flipping through the past's scrapbook, come join the present.

See your life just as you are right now. Face your single status and be responsible for yourself. The time in your life without a partner is the best time to explore what you want. All the precious limited resources are yours—time, money, effort, attention. And you can spend them just as you wish.

It can be uncomfortable. I flew to one of the most romantic cities alone, only to realize I had been running myself ragged. But I still remember that trip and am grateful for the (sleepy) adventure.

What adventures do you want to have?

What do you want your time with yourself to look like?

What do you like to do?

What brings you joy and makes you smile?

Asking those questions of yourself pays off. Think about all the time you spend thinking about what a past or potential partner might like or want. Now consider what can happen if you put that level of thought and effort toward learning to make yourself happy.

You are the star of the show. Solos do not last forever, but oftentimes they are a highlight. Think of being single as a moment in your life to be tackled in some practical, actionable ways, like your finances, social life, or how you choose to spend your time. But your solo is also a time to be savored, to show the world how you want to live your life and learn to love your own company.

Light pollution is when the bright lights of a city mask the night sky's wonders. Only if you take away the lights of the city can you appreciate the stars. When you dim the bright light of the comings and goings of romantic partners, or other distractions in your life, you make room to see the "stars" that will only shine for you in your solo.

Chapter Five

Sex in the Solo

Being single can mean taking a break from sex with a partner.

One option when you are not with a partner is to take a break from sex. Sex is a great place to hide or distract yourself from being single. The pursuit of casual sex can take away from the energy you want to be giving to yourself. Sometimes a sexless season is part of the process of getting to know yourself. If you commit to taking a break from sex, you can see where your mind wanders without partner sex in your life. You will get a different sense of your own sexual vibe and the ebb and flow and timing of your desire for sex. If you deny yourself something, you can experience and savor it in a new and different way.

Your next best sex could be with yourself. Masturbation. Enjoy! You are responsible for your own self-care, and masturbation is one of the most literal interpretations. If you are taking care of yourself to be your best, why should this be different? What percentage of people in sexually active partnerships are fantasizing during sex with their partner? Now you can just straight up enjoy those fantasies.

Masturbation can be a solution to being "horny." This situation is not exclusive to people without a partner. Don't imagine that all couples are having sex or having satisfying sex or only having sex with each other and you are not having sex at all. Coupled does not mean the sheets aren't cold.

Craving sex can also be about craving relaxation and sensuality. Of course, it's not the same, but a good deep stretch hot yoga class, blissing out and relaxing to great music, or taking extra time for bathing and lotion and climbing into fresh sheets can feel wonderfully sensual. I've had friends talk about working out being a release. Or getting a massage or dancing. Any of these can be avenues to sensuality.

Being single can mean exploring casual sex.

Another option when you are single and craving sex is to have sex casually. If an opportunity presents itself, or you wish to sample sex that's available to you outside of being in a relationship, go for it. In my experience, sex is one of life's great buffets. Grab a plate. Grab two. Keep yourself emotionally and physically safe. Keep your standards up. Wait for real chemistry and enjoy a lusty bit with just a few reminders:

> •No one ever slept their way into a good, solid relationship. Be honest and clear with yourself that building a relationship is one thing and play for play's sake is another.

> •Treat your mind and your private parts as very special places. Negative people or degrading incidents and critical reviews will not be tolerated. It's my experience that if you list "polite" as a must-have in a temporary partner, life between the sheets is much nicer.

45

• Only indulge when the suggestive invitation is met with enthusiastic and immediate consent — yours and the other person's. No waiting around for someone to think about it or clear the schedule or reach out when it works for you or them. Your solo sex standard should be enthusiastic consent. You can take it or leave it — and without enthusiastic consent and an easy meetup, leave it.

• The feel-good endorphins from a friendly adult romp (and the pre- and post-flirting) are a physical delight with a bit of an ego-boosting spring in your step. Both are terrific, but always remember your worth is way beyond what happens between your legs.

• Beware the feel-good chemicals produced during sex. It feels GOOD, and you can start having post-coital lovey-dovey thoughts with a casual partner, imagining, *Maybe we could be more.* I remind myself to readjust and just appreciate my fellow human for being my feel-good chemicals provider with a great in-bed manner.

• Sex as a grown-up requires a discussion of

fidelity, birth control, STD protection, and expectation of relationship parameters. Be very clear with yourself where you stand on these topics, then kindly and firmly share your feelings. Most importantly, listen carefully to your potential partner's response. Supportive and kind or not quite listening? Put yourself first.

Being single can mean being celibate.

Everyone is NOT doing it.

It is perfectly appropriate if this chapter does not speak to you, and you wish to keep your sex life private and within the confines of a committed relationship. If the thought of sex causes guilt or remorse or you're just not up for it in this season of your life, that's a great example of knowing yourself.

Being single can mean your next sexual encounter is unknown to you.

Perhaps you'll be in a happier solo place in your life and welcome your next sex partner in a new way which will lead to a better (sexier) connection. Maybe you'll learn about yourself and be ready to tell your next partner exactly how to make you very happy. How that happens is your journey, but *it is* possible. When you think about sex, I invite you to think about the *best* of what's possible.

Sex isn't just for the young and the nubile, reserved for love's first blush when everyone's hormones are crazy. As the years and decades go by, you make better partner choices. You accept your body more. You can better communicate your needs and wants. You realize there are not an endless number of sex partners. Love and connection can be tricky and short-lived, or long and less than inspiring, but having made and broken connections can help you appreciate sexy time when it comes your way. Experience can bring a new level of enjoyment and sweetness to getting to know a partner physically.

Here's another secret: maybe you have something you don't like about yourself or something a partner didn't like about you. Something physical that makes you insecure. For example, perhaps you hate your feet and are always wearing socks to cover them up. Your ex never wanted your bare toes on his side in bed. But someone new can come along and take one long look at ALL of you and say, "Baby, let's get you some sandals! I love those feet!" To paraphrase Shakespeare, the next beholder will see your beauty!

Your next sex could be your best sex. When your next partner appears in your life, that person could be the best sex of your life. Maybe all that other sex you've had until now was pretty good…but the next one will be even more amazing!

Chapter Six

Heal Grief

Sometimes it is sad events that bring you to your solo. As someone who is hurting, you can choose to heal with effort, hope, and resolve. That kind of emotional health is needed as you seek to build your best solo life. Wherever you are now does not have to be the story of your life. The next part of your story can be how awesome you made your solo.

To get the best result from *any* relationship, you have to be emotionally healthy. It's OK to pursue happiness in the now while you deal with overcoming a loss. Deciding to enjoy your solo can be done at the same time as any healing emotional work you are doing.

For example, having an injury is stressful. It affects everything in your life. You want to do everything in your power to not be hurting, but healing takes time. At the end of the day, you still watch movies and laugh with friends when you're sick. This concept applies to being single for unhappy reasons. Go to counseling. Read advice books. Journal. Becoming single can be a crisis and affects all parts of your life. That sadness, stress, and reorganizing of your life is serious work that needs to be done. Healing and rebuilding can be paired with considering your best solo life.

Healing is most important, but healing can take place at the same time as reading this book, giving time and energy to how you want your solo life to look and feel in a time when the crisis and hurt have passed.

I was at Mardi Gras in New Orleans where revelers of all ages lined the streets for colorful parades filled with music and fun. I was with a group of people celebrating a friend's fiftieth birthday and they were all staying together in a rented house. I travel for work all the time so I prefer a nice hotel room with points. Just as a couple might have a meal away from the group on vacation, one morning I took myself to brunch to enjoy my own company.

I bellied up to a barstool and debated oysters or crawfish while chatting with the gentleman next to me. He was a polished executive at the beginning of middle age in weekend attire. He shared that he was a recent widower. His wife had passed very suddenly, fairly recently, after they had a wonderful life together.

This guy had every reason to be sad. Yet here he was at Mardi Gras — happy parades, loud parties, and adult beverages. He talked about his travels, his favorite meals, and adventures since becoming single. He wasn't gleefully partying his way around the world and was clearly still in mourning. "I wouldn't choose this; I would choose to have her back," he said. However, that grief was separate from what he was going to do with his time to enjoy his life. And he was doing it solo. He was on vacation in New Orleans and going to parades and brunch alone determined to have a new life. What a success story on compartmentalizing grief and choosing activities and adventures that made him happy as a separate endeavor.

Allow me to share a lighthearted and more positive interpretation of the kinds of life events that may have brought you to your solo. These examples are intended to be irreverent to share another perspective on what could be in need of healing in your life.

He died.

I hosted a singles cruise on a fancy cruise ship. It was formal night. I met this lovely sixty-year-old woman in a beautiful ball gown draped in jewels. (Sidenote: I was with the rich people who have a lot of anti-aging money to spend. She could have been one hundred.) She looked fantastic and was on a beautiful vacation. A slow dance song came on and she was in tears. I asked about her husband and her eyes filled with tears again. She talked about their one-in-a-million love and how much her husband worshiped her and wanted her to have whatever she wanted. I quietly asked how long it had been since he passed.

Twelve years was the answer. Twelve years! Before I could stop myself in the neon light of the dance floor, I told her that I was literally an angel sent from heaven by her husband...who didn't want her to be unhappy! He certainly didn't want her to be crying in a nightclub!

Mourning is vital, but so is coming back to life.

He slept with someone else.

Maybe he did you a favor by showing you exactly who he is.

He never loved me./He was a criminal and slept with my sister.

You got the bad stuff out of the way and now your life is your own. Today you can take care of yourself and set yourself up to have a better time than you ever had with your ex!

No one has picked me. It's never worked out for me.

Divorce and the passing of a spouse are clear occasions for grief, but other life events that bring us to a new solo life can be subtler but still bring grief. It can feel like everyone else has graduated on to Real Life and you are stagnant staying single. Maybe you've dodged some bullets and not committed to someone who was not a good fit. Think of it as skipping the first unsuccessful marriage. Better an empty house than a bad tenant but yearning to be "chosen" and still being a single on simmer brings its own grief and working through to be more positive and accepting is valid healing.

I'm divorced—more than once. Two-time loser.

Jennifer freaking Aniston literally married the hottest movie star on the planet: Brad Pitt. Brad left her for another hot actress, Angelina Jolie, then Jen married another hot movie star. As of this writing, all four of these people are single. It happens. You can build a new life.

My husband became a woman.

Kris Jenner has really taken a beautiful lead on this one. I'm sure if you check her social media account right this minute, she's doing something fabulous. The father of her four children passed away from cancer in his fifties after defending O.J. Simpson. The husband of her last two children went from Olympian to becoming a woman. And Kris is certainly doing more than OK in a lot of categories.

If you are single and you are sad, I am sorry. Death, divorce, illness, crime, or breakups can lead to a single life you did not want. Grief, heartbreak, and loss can be horrible tyrants or great teachers. You deserve to mourn and grieve. Your first step is to address your mental and emotional health but leave your mind and heart open to create a new solo life you can love.

Chapter Seven

Closing Up Shop

Maybe you are hurt and angry about being single and someone gave you this book as a gift. You may have a million valid reasons why you do not have the time, money, or energy to be upbeat about being solo. This chapter is for you. Throughout this book I want to share positive stories and insights into being solo, but please know that I know there are extremely sad and terrible life events that lead to entering your solo hurt and burdened.

A close friend married her tall and handsome high school boyfriend a week after we graduated college. She had alcoholic parents in her adolescence and craved her own stable family, which is exactly what she got. Nestled in a perfect Midwest town out in the country, she had a sunny kitchen that opened on to a back porch with a shiny grill and a big backyard for two healthy children—a boy and a girl. The steps from the kitchen led to the carpeted dark basement with the only TV and computer in their family home. This is where her husband had a dark second life of crime and was sent to prison. My friend was a single mom—without child support—in a blink.

She had to take her children away from their father. She went to a small apartment filled with the giant responsibilities of making money and raising children. Putting one foot in front of the other, she did the work and dedicated five years to her children. Technically, she was single. But the topics in this book of filling your time positively and feeling good about being single weren't her concern. Her focus was entirely on being the only parent and provider. She would expend just enough focus (exercise and boundaries) on herself to be able to give as much as she could to raising her children.

She didn't spend extra money or time kicking back with a beer or thinking about dating or pondering enlarging her circle of friends. She was never negative or resigned to be alone forever. The fun adult part of her was simply given no energy. Those resources were used for two more important people in her life.

Somewhere around the five-year mark, her life changed. With the kids a little older and life much more certain, my friend took her own steps and built a new life. She moved to a house across the street from the city pool and a block away from downtown because she wanted to walk to adult fun as she envisioned living her empty-nest life in this new neighborhood. The backyard still has a grill but she's added kayaks, bikes, a garden, a hammock, and fire pit. All of which I've watched her work to provide herself for her enjoyment.

The point I'm making is that it's OK to close the shop. It's not OK to say it's going to be closed forever.

A solo season in your life can be like an ice cream store at the beach in winter. Sometimes it's just too cold for fun stuff like ice cream, but the shop is still there. After some time, when the weather is better, you can visit the store and try any flavor you want.

This example is extreme, but whatever circumstance

caused your pain is extreme to you. My point is that taking time after being hurt is OK—just don't close yourself down forever. Don't quite believe me? Think it'll be forever before you open your heart, I mean, the ice cream store? Trust me, there is fun and laughs and good times in the future.

Where you are today is not the end of your story! A broken heart can have more room for sweetness when you're ready to open the store.

Chapter Eight

Choose Your Thoughts

Your thoughts are powerful. Your thoughts are your responsibility. Look at how you feel about being single. Is being single something terrific and exciting? Are you being your best in your fleeting solo? Or is it a fate worse than...oh, I don't know, being with a lousy partner? There's a lot of gray area and it's easy to allow the negative to feel like the truth in singlehood. Or any stage of life.

There are ten million self-help books on the power of positive thoughts. Cognitive behavioral therapy is based on changing your thoughts to change your actions to improve your mental health. Please avail yourself of all that knowledge if you want to do better at having a positive outlook in life. Here we'll focus on thoughts about being in the solo.

I once had a very sad, teary Sunday afternoon when I realized I had owned my couch for seventeen years. It was an emotional shame spiral. Allow me to share the spiral, the translation, and the truth of my Couch Thoughts.

I thought: *This was the couch I bought for my single girl days, not my lifetime couch decision.*

Translation: Furniture marketers have told me I need a new couch every few years. Now I feel bad about myself.

TRUTH: It is a perfectly lovely, stylish couch.

I thought: *Couples are at Crate and Barrel bonding over couch selections and then probably having the time of their lives with their couches in their mansions with all the sex and problem-free lives they are leading.*

Translation: Grass is greener in a couple. Without a partner, I don't even have any grass to call green.

TRUTH: Can you imagine how long it takes a couple to pick out a couch? No one's life is problem-free. Chances are a partner is going to bring some furniture you don't quite love to a shared nest. Think about the wagon wheel table from *When Harry Met Sally.*

I thought: *All I have is this seventeen-year-old couch that I am probably going to die on alone.*

Translation: Being single translates to being alone forever and is a terrible fate.

TRUTH: Being single can end tomorrow. I could stay single for a long time. Both journeys can be happy.

Too much drama! Let's get to even another level of couch truth:

- It is a lovely couch. I picked it out myself. I also bought and paid for it myself.

- I have taken countless naps on this couch with the laundry undone and dishes in the sink. I have never awoken to a partner's snide remark or long-suffering sigh. I've just enjoyed my solo laziness judgment-free. This couch is also where I enjoy my own snacks and full power over the remote.

- I am healthy and well enough to enjoy my couch that is three feet from my full refrigerator, in my heated home, in my safe neighborhood, in my free country. Many blessings!

• Any moment Mr. Wonderful or Mr. Seems Wonderful Right Now could show up and that couch will experience even more awesome sexy time than it has in its history. Frankly, it has done pretty well in the sexy time category in my solo time!

• This couch has a future. Maybe I will put it in the servants' quarters when I buy my mansion after I find sunken pirate treasure on a scuba diving trip in Italy. Maybe it will decorate the nursery when I adopt children Angelina Jolie style. Perspective.

I used gratitude and hope and fantasy and fact to challenge my negative feelings about being single and turned around my thinking. And it feels a hell of a lot better than a shame spiral.

In marriage, you must be patient and give of yourself. You still must do that when you are single. You must be patient with yourself. You can observe your thoughts rationally and give yourself support. You can choose to speak to yourself kindly.

Commit to treating your mind like it is someplace very special. Negative thoughts (and people) and sad, lonesome self-talk are unwelcome.

Chapter Nine

Solo Life Vs. Partner Life

Comparison can kill a good time and a happy life. You cannot compare the worst parts of being single with the best parts of being in a couple. A partner will not solve all your problems. Please don't squint at the hedges that need to be trimmed and imagine a perfect landscaping partner. Who says you will hook up with a partner who will save you from gardening tasks? Next time you are headed to a social event alone, remind yourself that a partner may not socialize as you do, and in a partnership, your preferred fun outings may significantly decrease. Order from Uber Eats the way you want — no need to negotiate.

For so long I kept a mental list of all the experiences I didn't have because I was single. Over and over, I would sadly check them off in my head like fingering a knotty scar. What a waste of time that made me sad. I wish I would have allowed myself to feel those missing-out feelings, then done the work to apply some rational thought to that litany of things I was just so sure I was missing without a partner.

Here are a few examples of positive solo-eyed corrections of common single-life gripes:

I don't have anyone to snuggle on the couch to Netflix and chill.

You own the remote! No more history documentaries or ESPN (if that's not your thing)! No one's dissing your favorite reality show stars.

I'm alone on the holidays.

No in-laws!

I'm not sleeping with anyone.

Sleeping in a bed solo gives higher quality sleep, and if you don't know where your next sexual activity is coming from, maybe it'll be the best sex of your life. Living alone allows you privacy for anytime masturbation sessions. No nighttime temperature negotiation. No one's keeping you up. No one's extra blanket is making you hot.

I have to eat alone and cook for one.

You can eat wherever, whenever, whatever, and with whomever you want. No refrigerator to share. You don't have to avoid the big bag of Doritos that your partner can't live without. Or you can keep frozen cookie dough all to yourself. Heck, you can skip cooking and eat cereal every night.

I have to pay all my own bills.

You get your independence and to decide what makes you happy. You may even have time for a side hustle.

No one has ever gifted me jewelry or anything romantic.

Does the partner ever buy the wrong thing in this fantasy? Or worse, what if the wrong person gives you the right jewel? You can buy yourself anything you like! This applies to homes, flowers, perfume, vacations, lingerie, and just about anything else. If you want something, then you can have it.

Life seems empty and I have no future plans.

This is your life, and you are the star of it. You can have it be whatever you want to make it. You are in control of your happiness, no matter your marital status. You can choose to have it be about what you used to have or who used to be in it, or you can start enjoying your solo. It's hard to see the plans you may have had with a partner end, but you can make a new and better plan.

Use your intellect to overcome negative emotions. You are single right now, so challenge yourself to see the things that bother you about being single and visualize how you can better your approach. It's oh, so easy to daydream that life with a partner will be different. *If only some man would come along and kill all the spiders, or I had someone to cook for me.* Not all men are plumbers in the same way not all women are Betty Crocker, so it's best if each grown-up knows how to handle *all* of life's tasks adeptly. And just to add life perspective—single or coupled, *everyone* has to make dinner, do laundry, and pay taxes. With or without a partner, you'll have upswings and down days.

This "work" you have to do: being better, calling on your higher self, unraveling your emotions, facing and questioning your beliefs on your life without a partner— these tasks are very similar to the "work" you have to do to get along with someone in a relationship. Life is not a party; you have to work at it.

One final profound truth is that no matter what path you take in this life, you miss out on big things. I didn't have children, but I have traveled around the world. No road you follow will have every experience. Just be sure that whatever road you *are* on right now, you are making the most of it, and the road is leading you to where you wish to be.

Chapter Ten

Know Yourself to Be Selfless

My grandmother always said, "If you live alone, you get 'funny.'" What she meant is when you don't have anyone living with you, it can be easy to lose the skill of being adaptable and filling other people's needs first. You lose practice at getting beyond self. Being single means your life is all about you. Me! Me! Me! Myself! *Moi* and I.

You *can* certainly take that approach, but I'm not sure it will make you happy.

When you are single, you can spend all your time, effort, and energy meeting your every need, want, and whim. Volume always just right...only food you like...sleep when you wish...blow off or include anything you want. No pesky partner with their "feedback" or "suggestions." Yuck. This applies to your feelings too. When you live a solitary life, your feelings are the only ones you consider.

Since the only needs are yours, they can seem really important. One of the goals of making the best use out of being in your solo should be to get to know yourself. What a great gift your solo time gives you to get to know yourself better. However, sometimes, too much time considering exactly what you want and how to get it can make a person needy and hard to please. What we focus on grows, so say the Eastern meditation gurus. I find it to be true. If you look at your own needs and wants too intently for too long, they will increase. The more you consider only yourself, the harder it will be to satisfy yourself.

It's OK to have needs. We all do, and it's healthy and good to meet them. But if you allow your only focus to be yourself, and your list of details to be content becomes too complicated, you are out of balance. It can also make you selfish or self-absorbed. This is not the road to your best solo.

When you have your life just as you wish—your

schedule, your workout, your hobbies, your habits — you have a choice. You can become rigid and think, *Unless I follow the day as I always wish it to be, I will be unhappy and out of sorts.* OR you can say to yourself, *I am so comfortable and get to please myself endlessly, so when I* can't *have it my way, I will be the first one to be selfless.*

Over my years as a single woman, one of my value system commitments is I like to be aware of what life is like for people at all stages of life. I like to be a part of family life with children. You can't really have a catch-up at Starbucks with people under the age of eleven (and from ages eleven to twenty-three you are lucky if you get a couple sentences out of them). My solution? When I visit a family with small children, I sleep over. (The older kids I text. I spend half my life trying to find texts my nephews will think are cool.) I've slept in basements, the baby's room, and a sun porch just so I could be a part of life with some of my favorite families. Skipping a few nights in my big comfy single lady bed to get a close up on parent life and the little people? Worth it to me!

Voluntarily setting aside your comfortable routine to participate fully when you are with other folks has great payoffs. It builds your "you go first" muscle that can atrophy when living alone. You get exposed to how other folks are doing their day to day and enjoy the intimacy and company of others in the exact size dose of time you choose.

If you like to sleep late but the group gets going early, you can make it happen to go with the flow. You enjoy taking lots of time to get ready in front of the mirror, but when you are sharing a bathroom, hustle it. If you usually eat healthy but are spending time with kids in your life, skip or indulge in the chicken fingers. Be flexible.

Get beyond yourself. In your solo, you get to have your life just as you wish all the time, so when you get out there in the world, be ready to adjust. These are small adjustments in the grand scheme of things, but again, when you are single, that "sacrificing for the sake of others" muscle can atrophy. You must be sure to put yourself in situations to keep it strong. Fast-track to sacrifice: group travel, room sharing, and children of any size.

I was raised in a traditional family and can recall

being taught that a woman's goals should be: house, husband, baby. Find a man who will buy you a house and marry you and have a baby. As the times have changed, and my own path has not led to a husband and children, I began to think differently about this advice. The more I thought about this value from my childhood, my parents were telling me the way to be happy is to give of yourself to others. Be selfless.

As a spouse and parent, you are forced to put others first. As someone who is single, you must seek out situations to put others first. Without a built-in/live-in family structure, you have to find outlets in your life that are worthy of your time and effort. Another motivation to being selfless is how you want other people to see you. Do you want people to think you are selfish and fussy and hard to please?

If you are single, you can make so much of your existence about yourself and what you want and how you want it. And that's great, but the next step should be how you can contribute to others. The better you know yourself, the better you know how to make yourself happy. Since you have your life just as you wish, it should be *easier* for you to be flexible and giving. Yes, we all have preferences and likes and dislikes, but do not allow yourself to become selfish, and demanding. Instead, think of being single as being able to give more when it's with the people you care about.

Chapter Eleven

Feeling Lonely
Use T.R.A.P.S. and S.P.A.R.K. Yourself

As a solo ship in the sea, you control where you set your sail. I would argue you are powerful enough to control the weather that calms or calls those seas, but one unavoidable swell is you feeling lonely. Perhaps surprisingly this is one of the later concepts I chose to include in this book. Loneliness is part of the human condition. It is not exclusive to those not in a romantic partnership.

Those lonely feelings will come to us all. Maybe it's a feeling that just comes. Maybe it is prompted by a time of the week or an interaction or something you read or saw on TV. As a Family of One, you can respond positively to loneliness. When those times come, take the following steps. I suggest you use the different methods of T.R.A.P.S. to endure loneliness.

Take Time to Be Thankful

Take out a sheet of paper and write down one hundred things you feel grateful for. You have paper and a pen and can read, write, and think. There's your first five on the gratitude list — ninety-five to go. You can also write down all the people you love who love you. Think of happy times in the past and future plans while reminding yourself that a little loneliness between happy memories and whatever is coming next is an OK place to be. Remember, your life can change for better or worse in an instant, so appreciate the present.

Reach Out for Connection

A problem shared is a problem halved. I often find just calling someone and saying my emotions aloud helps them dissipate. You can also reach out to someone in your life and share yourself. And there's no better way to get over your own sad emotions than to reach out to someone else who needs love and support. A good way to get love is to give it.

Act and Distract

Take a walk. Play music. Watch something funny on TV. Take a bath or shower. Bake a cake. Sing a song. Run an errand. Clean something. Make some stuff dirty. Change your focus to something that fills your attention. Hit all those senses. This may seem simple, but a few YouTube laughs and a couple check marks on your to-do list can work wonders.

Peace and Prayers

Not feeling that energetic? Those lonely feelings that happen down deep in the quiet and the dark are also a place to find peace. Meditate. Journal. Rest. Know that this too shall pass. Experiencing the low times will help you enjoy the good times.

Stop the Spiral

Everyone feels lonely. You are not lonely based on

your age, size, smarts, or circumstances. Loneliness happens in high schools and nursing homes, at size 2 and 22, for the rich and poor and everyone in between. Recognize loneliness as a just a feeling and not a permanent state.

T.R.A.P.S. is a good approach for *bouts* of loneliness.

If you feel *chronically* lonely, you need to learn how to enjoy your own company and fill your time with relationships and activities that make you happy. That's an inside job. Only you can build a life that feels full to you. Good news! You're reading the right book to help you build a solo that fits you! To avoid a continually lonely life, I suggest you check for a S.P.A.R.K.

Schedule Your Life

Look at your time spent with yourself and fill it with activities you enjoy! Loneliness is more likely if you listlessly allow life to happen to you.

People Are Fallible

It's easy to be disappointed by others and to feel left

84

out. People are busy or distracted or handling their own challenges. It's rare that people are purposely isolating you. I promise.

Accept and Allow

Accept yourself and allow yourself to be yourself. The more peace you feel with who you are and your life circumstances, the less isolated you will feel. If you want to make positive changes, that's great, but one of the gifts of a solo is getting to know and love yourself.

Respond To Others

Smile! Open doors! Make eye contact. No matter who reaches out to you in big and small ways, respond always. Do you have unanswered emails or calls or texts? Put yourself out there and always be responsive. If you are invited to something, go! If you are interested, show up! Become a regular at a coffee place or the library or church and find community.

Know Yourself

Put a lot of effort into knowing what makes you happy. What kinds of friends? What kinds of interactions? What kinds of activities? Do you need big, loud social events with lots of people or just a nod hello from a neighbor? Do you long to be understood with intimate conversations with longtime friends or do you just want company for a few activities?

Lonely feelings are scary and difficult and occasionally a part of being human. Everyone has been and will be lonely in this life, so the solo is a very good time for you to learn what makes you lonely and how you respond best when you feel those lonely feelings.

Chronic loneliness is a serious situation. I want you to value yourself enough to decide that you will work on the concepts in this chapter. If you were hungry, you wouldn't just accept that it's your lot in life to be hungry all the time and you'll just suffer. You must make the choice that you will seek a solution to a lonely life.

Meanwhile, one person's lonely is another person's beloved alone time. How much and what kind of interaction you need to not feel lonely in this life can only be determined and brought into your life by you.

Chapter Twelve

Rituals and Routines

It can be easy to let time pass. *It's just me… I'm not dating anyone right now… No plans this weekend… Sigh. I'm by myself. Who cares?* That's boring! Get yourself some enjoyable day-to-day rituals. What do you crave? Comfort or adventure? Rest or action? What lights you up? Being with people? Beautiful vistas? City settings? The natural world? What feels good? Checking off your to-do list? Hustling? Quiet time?

Maybe you feel good about being single most of the time. You have a job, friends, and family that keep you busy. Still, there are lonely or emptier times when you really notice being single or that make you sad. Observe yourself and when these kinds of emotions surface for you. Don't let these times come and just endure them.

Plan ahead. Think about what would make you happy, then pursue that. Knowing what triggers you to feel sad or lonely allows you to strategize to avoid or distract or comfort yourself, and that is doable and powerful.

Christmas.

I was never a big fan of Christmas — too much family chaos along with the holly jolly when I was a kid. Long ago, I committed to do what *I* wanted over Christmas, so I have had all kinds of non-traditional Christmases traveling or just staying in and not participating. If done right, it's very relaxing and easy on the pocketbook.

Mornings.

Don't like waking up alone? Start doing a few yoga stretches right out of bed as a way to be good to yourself instead of lying and stewing and feeling lonesome. Make your morning coffee time a time to veg out to TV for thirty minutes before you face the day. There are many morning meditations or motivational videos you can find online if you wake up feeling a little too solo.

Saturday Night.

One glimpse of Facebook and it feels like the whole world is in a party dress and sipping champagne. They are not. Saturday night can be for chores, studying, reading, or hobbies. If you work a 9 to 5, Monday to Friday job, Saturday night is your time. Go out solo early on Saturday night. I have a favorite "hot" restaurant in Chicago, and I love to sit at the bar at five on Saturday night and watch the crowd as the place begins to fill up. I'm happily home and in my comfy pajamas by eight.

Sundays.

A wise friend of mine once said what you do on Sunday morning is really who you are. It's not necessarily a social time, but it can be. Church only lasts an hour or two, then you have yourself to entertain. What a lovely gift each week. I knew one friend who would just listen to jazz on the radio every Sunday.

Sunday nights

. The work week is coming. The fun weekend is over.

Make a ritual of washing your sheets, taking a bath, and climbing into bed early. I have a standing Sunday night dinner at a friend's house. It's a great way to avoid the "Sunday Scarys" of thinking about starting a new week.

Too Quiet Times.

Does the time feel different when your kids are away from you? Or is there some time of the week that reminds you of your ex or your breakup? Identify that time and decide if keeping yourself busy is best, or if taking time to sort through the emotions that come up in the quiet times is better.

Valentine's Day

Is it only for couples? I attended a bachelorette party for a friend of a friend and watched the darling bride-to-be open a seduction candle. I knew this particular bride had a *very* active sex life and I thought to myself, *I could use a seduction candle — I'm single!* Then it hit me. I was going to host my own bachelorette party every year on Valentine's Day.

I invited lots of fun ladies (regardless of marital status) to my house. I told them all to bring a racy, raunchy, or romantic gift, then we played one of those gift exchange games so everyone ended up with a surprise. The invite told everyone to wear sexy red. The menu had playfully naughty themes. There was an "all ball" appetizer menu one year. Only women were invited to my house, then we went to the second stage of the party at a bar where guys were invited. Have you ever walked into a party of waiting guys and you are the host bringing a giant group of ladies dressed in red and clutching their sexy gift? It's amazing. My well-promoted theory was that Valentine's Day can also celebrate the chase for love! One final note: the décor at the bar was wall-to-wall strings of colorful ladies' underwear! Happy Valentine's Day!

Chapter Thirteen

Friends and Socializing

Having love and deep connection and healthful interactions in your life does not demand a partner. Those connections come from all kinds of friendships. Build a social network. An actual, IRL social network, not one built on swipes and likes. Making new friends isn't confined to the third grade or freshman year at college, the geography of the street you live on, or your colleagues at work. It's a lifetime process.

The MIT Age Lab created three questions to assess if an elderly person is isolated:

1. Do you have someone you can call and go get an ice cream cone with on a warm summer night?

2. Do you have someone you can call if you can't

reach a light bulb that needs to be changed?

3. Do you have someone to go with you to a pre-planned lunch?

I think these questions are also an excellent starting point to look at the life you are building around yourself and assess your own friendships.

If your day-to-day life goes downhill, who do you have? Or better yet, if your ship is sailing along beautifully, who is joining you out on the high seas? Be sure you get (and give) love and support and companionship in life. This is something we all must do to thrive, no matter our relationship status. And a partner can't serve your every need, so having a full life — solo or coupled — is about investing in friendships. Making new friends requires generosity of self and listening and active questioning. This is a terrific way to keep your intimacy muscles sharp even if you are not in an intimate relationship.

The cast of *The Golden Girls*, *Friends*, *Seinfeld* — heck, even all those doctors on *Grey's Anatomy* — seem to have endless friend interactions daily. Popular culture promotes Friendsgiving — gathering with your chosen family of friends the Saturday before you spend actual Thanksgiving with your biological family. Having a tribe of ride-or-die friends is always on trend, but it's OK if your friendships don't look like popular TV as long as you feel your needs are met. Ice cream, light bulbs, and lunch are really good questions. Maybe you have a gaggle of friends since childhood or just a few close pals. Know that being your best at being solo is taking a regular look at your friendships.

I have two pieces of very good news about being single and making friends. First, you have more time to be a better friend. Second, you can be friends with all kinds of different people. One great way to know yourself better is to get to know others. And that wholeheartedly includes folks of the other gender and lifestyles and ages and status. Be open.

If you live alone and make your own schedule, you can be a more flexible friend. Change your schedule to walk during naptime for the new mama friend. Have a friend who is starting a business or passionate about a volunteer pursuit? Give an afternoon of your time to help that friend reach a goal. Have friends who play or follow a sport you're not familiar with? Go spectate. Without a partner, you can go and participate and depart. It's a little simpler in a social setting to be "just" one instead of one plus one, and that can make your solo life experiences so much richer. Maybe a friend is hosting family and needs an extra hand. If you like that kind of thing, why not help out? As a solo person in a solo life, you have the opportunity to extend yourself more in your friendships and social interactions.

Being single also allows you to fit into different groups of friends. I had an annual vacation with three friends from high school and their spouses to a beautiful cabin on a lake in the woods, and year after year I got to be everyone's friend. Yes, I was with three families and I was sleeping solo in a twin bunk bed in my forties. But on the upside, I got to participate in all the activities with all the different groups on the vacation.

When the guys went golfing, I was their fourth. When the moms went to happy hour as a break from getting the kids ready, I joined as one of the gals. I can sleep in anytime, so I chose to be up early with the little kids without their parents, which can be pretty fun. Did I get to visit with each person—kid and adult—one on one? Yes! I didn't have to negotiate vacation childcare with my spouse or try to reconnect with friends while entertaining my partner who was just going along with my group of friends.

I also got to slip away for a nap or an hour of reading anytime I wanted!

Did I have an extra glass of wine on arrival night when I faced my married with children peers and I was rolling solo? Sure. How could I help but compare? We all started in the same place and they ended up with traditional families. But that comparison also allowed me to appreciate my single life. Freedom to build my own life, choose how I spend my time and money and energy to be a great aunt and friend!

As a singleton, feedback from your friend community can be louder than it should be. Maybe your friendships are long standing or intense, just like a committed romantic relationship, but you didn't necessarily commit to a friend's value system and influence in your life the way you would thoughtfully commit to a partner. If you want to change or grow, sometimes people in your life are slow to see you a new way. I would argue you can widen your circle anytime and you never know what new groups are open to you or what's around the corner.

When I was a tour director leading trips for singles, I hosted a weekend in Chicago. It had been a successful trip, and on Sunday morning, I was talking with one of the attendees. He was a quiet, middle-aged, regular guy, and he said, "I'm from a small town and I've been in the same relationship for a long time. She dumped me for someone else. Everyone in my town knew about it." I could tell he had been hurt and embarrassed. Then he shared that he came on this singles trip and met all these people who don't know anything about his ex or her new guy or his town. He openly admitted that he didn't really know this kind of fun with new people was out here and that he had forgotten what it's like to make friends. As a newly single person, he was able to choose a new experience and was exposed to a whole fresh group of people who gave him a positive reflection of himself.

Keep an open mind when it comes to friends. Know that when it comes to friendship during the solo time of your life, you may have more to give and you might be able to connect with different types of folks. And that can make life so much richer!

Chapter Fourteen

The Cocktail Party Question

Imagine yourself out socially and being singled out for being single. The invasive cocktail party question has kept many a good person away from a good time. The cocktail party question is when you feel cornered and questioned about your single status. You think, *I would go, but they'll ask me about the divorce, and I just can't face it*. Or, *Everyone is going to ask if I'm dating someone or why don't I have a date*. Or, *Questions about my breakup are just too hard for me right now*.

Facing a social event when you don't feel great about being single is hard. It feels like the whole world is conspiring to highlight the one fact about yourself you feel bad about. It can make you nervous for days in advance of the event. You worry about running into someone from your day-to-day life when you are feeling shaky about being single.

Go to the party anyway. Now this is something that is easy to say and hard to do. But it is the road to connection and healing. Even if you fear being asked about your solo status, say hi when you see people you know. Remember, no one is thinking about you enough to judge you as harshly as you might be judging yourself.

You think people will be shocked, disapproving, disappointed, or judgmental. As with any insecurity, ask yourself, *Is anyone really thinking that much about me?* More importantly, if they *are* interested, it is most likely with positive intent. Marital or relationship status is a basic question; it's not a criticism or a jab.

Quieting the noise of your insecurity regarding your solo status and sharing your truth allows you to see others clearly. As you strategize how to respond to questions about your single status, know that it's possible to preserve your feelings and increase intimacy and support from people. You can choose to kindly and succinctly share that you are having a romantic challenge or a change in marital status and most people will be supportive.

There's a TV personality on *The Real Housewives of New York City* named Luann de Lesseps, who is lovely and refined. She literally is a countess of some kind of royalty. She divorces and happily dates a young and handsome Frenchman. They break up. There's a scene where Luann is at a swanky rooftop social event and she is dressed beautifully. Someone comes up and inquires about her date. She replies, "We broke up and I'm really sad about it." Direct and honest. She's in a party setting and her facial expressions, tone of voice, and her actual words show that she is sad, but she acknowledges it. Most admirably, she has gotten herself to a party and is still having a fun social time while navigating a breakup.

Just so you have them, here's a list of ready to go responses:

- "Oh. I'm single."

- "Still looking."

- "One frog closer to the prince every day."

- "Overqualified for marriage."

• "Happily divorced."

• "I used to be married."

• "Flying solo these days."

• "I keep looking! Fate must have someone wonderful waiting for me."

• "I'm a widower."

• "Having some pretty terrific new sex with some fun candidates. Stay tuned."

• "Turns out the last one and I weren't a match. Looking forward to the next one."

You can say any of these responses, then just leave it and change the subject. You don't have to explain, defend, or give details.

Facing socializing after a rough loss is hard. Here's another way to think of it. What if you were injured? Imagine you had a broken leg that was healing—like if you are healing from a breakup—and you walk into a party with a big cast and a limp and someone said, "Hey, how's your leg?" Would you think, *Who are they to ask about my leg? Like my cast makes me an outcast?* (Pardon the pun!)

You might say, "Yes, I'm injured. I've been laid up. It's frustrating and limiting, so I'm crabby, but I'm going to get better."

And the other person would empathize. "Oh, I've broken my leg. It's hard." Or they might say, "Broken legs are common. I hope you're doing OK."

They are a nice person.

Or they might say, "Whoa, you broke your leg? Your awesome leg? You'll never walk right again, I bet. How are you going to cope? I always thought you walked funny, so I'm not surprised your leg is broken."

And now you know that someone who asks questions like that is *not* a nice person.

A breakup can be similar to that broken leg. It will heal, and in most social settings, people will be caring. Anyone who is kind is asking about your marital status to get to know you better, or to support you, not to judge you.

Chapter Fifteen

Allies

If you are doing life together with a partner, you double the areas of expertise and the amount of time and abilities to get things done. A duo, simply put, gets more done. Maybe she cooks and he does the yard. There are a million other examples of splitting the chores and tasks that are life. When you are single, you have to solve every problem yourself. This can feel disheartening and lonesome. *Or* you can choose to see the world filled with people who are your potential allies with all kinds of strengths.

An ally is a kind of friend. It's a partnership that shares resources and capitalizes on strengths. Maybe it's a person who you pay for a service, but you interact with them in a way that they go a little extra for you. Maybe it's a friend of a friend and you ask for an introduction.

People love to be asked for advice. People want to share their passions. Sometimes being single can cause decision fatigue. Having every single detail of a project or just your life up to you can be exhausting. Your energy to execute the best choices can diminish. You can make every single frigging decision on your own or you can reach out to someone with more expertise or interest and enlist them as your ally.

The first key is to pick someone who is enthused about your question or task. The second key is to be known as the kind of person who shows appreciation and is ready to give back when asked to call upon *your* strengths to help someone else. The ally approach only works if you are a fountain, not a drain in this life. You can't be a user, or would-be allies will run from or resent you.

I am not an expert on every topic or even interested in being an expert on every topic, so I have all kinds of people smarter than me who I regularly ask for advice. Sometimes I just hand over whatever I am trying to figure out.

Need to fill out the work football pool? I send it right on over to a friend's husband with the season tickets and weekly ten-year tailgate tradition who knows I'll bring baked goods next time I'm at the same game. Anything with the car? Ask the older man down the street who is always out cleaning his roadster, then follow up his opinion with the mechanic someone else I trust recommended. Old man gets a friendly wave and a follow-up where I give him all the credit. The mechanic gets me as a loyal customer who knows how to ask questions based on whatever info I got from the neighbor with the roadster.

The same woman has cut my hair for twenty years. Occasionally I will say something like, "Are the kids cutting it shorter these days?" and *poof* I have a spring bob at exactly the right time of year. She literally makes all the hair decisions. I hand her my phone to tell me what shampoo to buy on Amazon.

I once had a fire in my condo and had to deal with the insurance. It was a scary and complicated process to do alone. I asked around my inner circle for help and my friend's husband's brother was an arson investigator who I had met at a few social events over the years but never knew his profession. I called him a few times over the course of getting back to normal and received terrific advice. If I had a partner, would I have taken the extra step to find such a comforting expert? Probably not, and I would have missed out.

I had an experience with a relative who was showing signs of scary mental health issues and I was freaked out. I didn't want any of my friends or family to join my freak-out if it wasn't warranted, so I wrote a venting email, then I slept on it. In the morning, I looked through my contacts for someone to send it to — kind of a backward approach. I remembered a friend from high school who was a physician with expertise in the exact problem I was facing. I shortened up my venting and sent it off, and received a kind and quick response addressing my fears and sending me best next steps. I had maybe seen this lady twice in as many decades. But she came through in her response and support.

The handyman lives in my building. Any home repair decisions to be made are all him. Thank you notes and baked goods go along with the cash payment for him. Scary termites? I ask the neighbor with the nicest yard what he does about his termites, then nod my head until he says, "I think I have some of the spray left. I'll come over." Post spray at my place, he leaves with a bottle of wine. Once I was on a short timetable to move a relative into a rehab hospital. That person made a specific request for a really good reading lamp. Out of the blue, I emailed an engineer friend the request and he sent me an Amazon link for a great reading lamp. That was a year ago and I've since bought that lamp for a bunch of different people. It was easy for my friend to do and way better than I could do myself! What's a challenge for you might be very easy for someone in your circle, and it is very much OK to ask for help.

My financial advisor, real estate agent, and fitness trainer are all smart, handsome younger guys. What lady, single or otherwise, doesn't want that in her life? Are they real friends? No, it's their job, but they are true allies, and our connection is genuine. You can cultivate a friendly and mutually beneficial way to handle tasks that might go to a partner. Never be afraid to ask for help or an introduction.

Want to run a 5K? Check Facebook and see who is already out there running and let them know the race you want to sign up for and ask their opinion. Planning to travel somewhere new? Ask someone who has visited already. Picking furniture or paint colors? There's someone in your life who loves the interior design world. Find them. Making a health decision? Get online and join a chat group. Approach people with a simple request for information and allow them to jump in and offer more help or not. It is not being a burden if you allow people plenty of room to decline.

There's a secondary benefit to approaching people in your life as allies. Lots more places feel welcoming. I travel a ton, so the mailman and I are buddies because he holds the mail for me. If I've been traveling too long, the guy who runs the little food store in my condo building comes out from behind the counter to "get a good look at you." Just like an adopted uncle in my neighborhood! I always thank the Starbucks people in my neighborhood when I set up my laptop for hours, nursing my venti ice water, and it sure feels homier. The Greek dry cleaner enjoys my debate about his prices, so that means clothing pickup includes a chat. Favorite topic? People we know who are Greek.

Looking at all the folks in your life as allies is a terrific way to bring lots of people into your solo world. As an extrovert, I easily reach out to folks and connect. If that's not your style, another approach is to make a list of areas in your life you wish you had someone in your circle who could give you solid advice or support or expertise. Next make a list of your friends and family and start asking. "Mom, do you know someone in real estate?" "[College roommate], do you know a headhunter?" The world is smaller than you think. Reach out!

Chapter Sixteen

Get an Idiot Mirror

We are all human, so from time to time, each one of us will act like an idiot. Therefore, we all need a sounding board or a person who can help us find ourselves again, or what I like to call an idiot mirror. An idiot mirror is a trusted and truthful friend you can ask to help sort out situations where you (or someone else) are being an idiot. This is the kind of compass we all sometimes need to get back to our best self.

By definition, an idiot is a stupid person. I do not believe in name calling, but we are all going to act or interact with someone being an idiot...oftentimes ourselves.

We all need help finding perspective from time to time. Idiotic behavior can be very hard to sort out. If you allow yourself to be alone with your thoughts, it is so easy for situations to become overblown in your own interpretation. Your feelings are happening to YOU, so it makes them difficult to interpret. Just like a mirror, situations may appear bigger than they actually are! Sometimes you are so close to an idiotic mistake that you can't see it.

For example, when you are acting like an idiot and don't quite know it yet. Maybe some of your life practices are not great. Maybe you start to think eating six donuts on the way to work is not helping your attempts at working out. Maybe it is a dead-end job you are in and you haven't quite found a way to commit to finding a new one. Self-reflection is better when someone else helps you interpret the reflection you see. Having someone in your life who knows and loves you enough that you can go to them and ask, "Am I being an idiot in this situation?" is invaluable.

An idiot mirror is also good when you know you've acted poorly, and you are certain you have done so in front of the entire world. Maybe you were out with friends with too many cocktails placed in front of you and you danced on a table at a Denny's. But it was during breakfast and that kind of thing is frowned upon. You feel just terrible and are certain the whole world saw and shared your actions—probably with its own hashtag, #thedennysdancer. Yikes. Call your idiot mirror friend to remind you that it really wasn't *that* terrible. Everybody overdoes it now and again. The world will keep turning. For "danced on the table at Denny's" you can easily substitute situations like, yelled at someone who didn't deserve it, cried at the mall and scared the Sephora lady, or any number of emotional outbursts which are better known as being human but can feel really embarrassing.

For example, I had a tough travel day just before Christmas—my least favorite holiday—and very unkindly took it out on the baggage claim person as I filed a lost bag report. Later I was ashamed that I had been so petty, and my cousin/idiot mirror said, "There's only one perfect person in this world and we celebrate his birthday on Christmas." She didn't say, "Oh! That was bad," or, "Why did you do that?" She gently reminded me that our faith allows for mistakes. She did not criticize, pile on, or excuse the behavior. She gave perspective I couldn't find myself.

Another hard-to-see-in-yourself kind of idiocy is when your mind is obsessing over something. Every single choice your sister is making about her wedding is driving you mad. It's all you can talk about. Your ex has a new partner and it's on social media. You are checking that feed more often than The Weather Channel waiting for a snow day. You truly dislike one of your coworkers and from the snacks he brings to work to his insufferable (and predictable) "let's circle back" call-ender, you are paying more attention to him than your job.

This is where your idiot mirror would reflect to you the number of times you've revisited details of these situations, then ask why they bother you so much. And point out maybe it's best for you if you don't let them bother you so much. This usually leads to addressing these situations with biting your tongue or taking a break from Instagram.

When someone has been an idiot toward you, an idiot mirror can help too. Talking about being hurt and specifically naming your negative feelings is incredibly powerful. A problem shared is a problem halved. Sometimes it's enough to say something aloud to dispel its power over us. Once I was leading a work team and found a caricature drawing of me. It was a dead-on resemblance and, *yikes*, not flattering. After dialing my eyebrow wax lady for an appointment and silently committing to get to the gym more often, I felt hot tears come to my eyes. I took the mean-spirited drawing to a friend. He took a long look at it, then looked at me, smiled, and said, "Well, they really did capture you." He said it so kindly. And he was right. I have faults and they were captured in black and white. His light and supportive tone immediately took the sting out of the situation and gave me back my perspective. His reaction helped me see that the picture of me was just drawn by…some idiot.

How to find an idiot mirror? Choose someone who knows you and loves you and will tell you the truth with kindness. Someone who wants the best for you will take a minute and assess what your situation is and properly identify the idiot in any given situation.

We all have the kind of friend who is dying to tell us

the truth with a very healthy helping of his or her opinion, but perhaps not in the nicest tone or word choice. It's great to be able to have the insight and courage to call a spade a spade. But do you really need to call it a shit shovel? You also don't want someone like your mother or another relative who thinks everything you do is just wonderful (or awful, depending on your relationship). Your idiot mirror can't blindly think everything you do is great.

You can't ask someone who doesn't share your values. If you have a friend who thinks tossing back a few and dancing on tables just isn't ladylike or ever appropriate and you call that kind of behavior "a good Saturday night," that's not a good fit.

There's another big secret to successful idiot mirroring. You have to be open to really seeing what's in your mirror. Work on yourself to be open to feedback and communicate that openness to people in your life you trust. To be and face idiots is very human. We all have idiot situations in our lives. Facing what's in the mirror lessens their power.

Chapter Seventeen

Beware the Friendly Distractions

Friends and allies are healthy, wonderful, and important parts of any life, but sometimes too much of a good thing can be a distraction. To have your best go at being single, you must accept being solo and appreciate your life for what it is—and what you can make it on your own. This requires space to really be single and not allow distractions to swallow all your time and energy. Investing time in yourself and your solo will bring you rewards that are hard to see coming when you are newly single.

Distractions are often wonderful parts of our lives that we try to use to fill the place of a partner in an unhealthy way. If you allow a distraction to steal your energy, smudge your view of yourself, or block you from exploring your own feelings and experiences being solo, it is a mistake. You have to really be alone to decide how you want being alone to look and feel in your life. Seek to find a balance between enjoying the good parts of your life while having boundaries and investing the time and space in building your solo.

I was working as a tour guide leading singles through Italy one summer. Just before I left home, I went on a pretty good first date with a handsome Italian American doctor. As I traveled through Italy, I had daily giant fantasies about marrying this doctor and going to Italy on our honeymoon. We would probably bring his parents to Italy someday. All the things we learned and experienced in Italy we would bring home to our beautiful Italian-inspired mansion we had together as a married couple. I spent hours and hours on this detailed fantasy. The date had been, what, three hours? Why did I not open my eyes and simply enjoy that Italy trip? Maybe interact with actual people, not my fantasy Italian husband.

Daydreaming is lovely. Spinning too much of a tale based on such a fleeting meeting is not so good. That's a friendly distraction. It's a thought filler that steals the enjoyment of your actual present.

Here are some relatable examples:

Your Colleague or "Work Husband"

You have so many inside jokes. There's lunch every day and a shared coffee order. You have a routine together. He understands what annoys you and what your goals are. If he likes a TV show or a book, you are sure to watch or read it too. You see each other every day. There's always so much to talk about. He always sides with you. You work forty hours a week, but you deserve someone who is part of all the hours of your week.

The Trainer

He cares that you get enough nutrition and sleep. He really tracks your activities and wants you to reach your goals. The time you spend together is super focused and mostly on you! You see each other very consistently, so there's always the next time to look forward to. He says so many positive things about your body and he'll schedule as many sessions as you want. You're so busy tracking macros and counting reps, who has time for a social life?

The Ex or a Crush

You know everything about them. You think about the times you've had together…or dream of how it could be or how it should have been. In your imagination you rehearse conversations in all kinds of probable and improbable situations. You definitely keep an eye out for where his car is parked. When you measure all the mental energy you are expending against the actual interactions you are having, are you coming up way short? A crush can crush you and an old flame can burn.

The One That Got Away

You can remember your time together so clearly and happily. It is easier than you thought to find so many details about him online. When you think about him, it's like you could have predicted where he is now. When you are with people who know you both, you find all kinds of reasons to bring his name up in conversation. And from what you can guess from what you know, he's probably open to rekindling so many happy times when he really made you feel wonderful. Fantasies are fun, but they are just that: fantasies.

A textual relationship

Your phone is always pinging! No detail too small to report in via text and the texts happen at all hours. Be sure there's a balance of in person IRL (in real life) time in any relationship.

Your Pet

You plan your schedule around their schedule. You will cancel plans with people to get home and be with them. You cuddle and snuggle. He always makes you laugh. You have a million pictures of him. No matter your mood or what kind of treatment you dish out, he keeps coming back for more every time like he loves you the most in the world. Furry friends are wonderful, but stay open to human friends too.

Your Married-with-Children Friend or Sister

Being an aunt is the best! But it's time to take a second look if you find yourself thinking any of these thoughts:

- I'm like the second mom.

- I'm over at their house so often because they just get me.

- Her husband is so the third wheel. What do they even have to talk about when I'm not around?

The truth is you are not the parent and boundaries are a good thing.

Your Children

You meet all their needs with all your time. They couldn't go on without you. They are your only focus. Family time is the best time, down to Saturday nights and snuggling in bed. Sometimes you want to feel like you're a kid too. But that's your children and they WILL grow up and have their own lives. Will you have your own life when that happens?

Don't get me wrong; it's great to have family and friends and colleagues and pets. It's wonderful to be friends with the trainer and the greatest calling to be a parent. Those are all wonderful parts of a full life! It's not great to give all of your time and effort outside yourself. No matter how worthy the recipient.

There is so much good in a solo life, but you have to be brave enough to set healthy limits in other parts of your life instead of escaping living solo. Your head and heart spaces are precious. Hold onto some for yourself.

This is a leap of faith. You have to give up over-occupying yourself, which can be lonely and scary. Choose to put yourself first. If you let yourself be distracted, you are accepting crumbs from the table at the banquet. Allowing any part of your life to overgrow and overshadow you building your solo life is accepting less than you deserve. Examine your relationships. Are any of them using you and not giving enough back?

Chapter Eighteen

Party for One: Staying In

We all have downtime. A night off, a Sunday morning, or a holiday weekend. Sometimes you have no plans...with another person. With an attitude adjustment and some planning, you can turn even everyday chores and errands into a Party for One.

Yes, you can just flop on your couch and scroll through Netflix with an internal soundtrack of "All by Myself" in your head like that iconic singleton Bridget Jones. You can gloomily roll through your usual to-do list week after week. When it's just you, it can be easy not to pay attention to the time you have to yourself.

It's even easier to be negative: *I'm always alone. Activities are only fun with a partner or other people. Why motivate?*

Fast-forward to the end of your solo time the next day or Monday morning. How do you want to feel? Like you can't even remember where the time went? That your life is just boring and lonely? Or like you have chosen to make yourself the guest of honor at a Party for One.

Just because you are alone doesn't mean you should allow your free time to fritter away into the void of pajama clad social media scrolling and snacking. First step? Increase your anticipation and planning. Anticipation is part of the enjoyment of your time with yourself. Just like you would anticipate time with a partner or friend. A little advanced planning makes sure you spend your time as you wish. Your downtime in your solo is precious and fleeting.

When approaching an evening or a weekend alone, think of it as a big break for yourself. Ask any parent with young children or anyone with a demanding schedule. Who doesn't want a big old break? Challenge yourself to flip off the mental switch from feeling alone and partner-less to appreciating where you are today — a single adult able to enjoy your own company with free time to spare.

If you reset your attitude, that night alone on the couch is a perfectly worthy choice of how to spend time with yourself. Wait to watch your favorite show until you have a few episodes saved and free time. Pour yourself a glass of whatever you like, serve up something delicious, and climb onto your couch and enjoy the remote all to yourself!

Respect your time with yourself enough to anticipate and plan to make your solo time fun and rewarding. Here are a few scenarios to get your inner Party for One Planner inspired:

Healthy Party for One

You could just hit the gym and go to bed, but that's uninspired and boring. Instead, think of it as an opportunity to take extra time with your workout. Try a machine or a class you can't always fit in. Add a sauna or a steam. Plan to have a post-workout meal full of something healthy and maybe read or watch something that gets you inspired for more healthy habits.

Dining Party for One

Don't eat cereal over the sink if that doesn't make you happy. Not having a partner or a crowd is no reason not to cook if you love to cook (or eat!). Invest in your health and enjoyment and make the effort to feed yourself well. Make soup or Sunday sauce. You can freeze extra. Roast a chicken or a ton of vegetables. Bring them out of the oven and serve them to yourself beautifully presented. You can eat them while you watch the Food Network, and you can always eat the leftovers your favorite ways in the next few days. There are quite a few cookbooks ingeniously dedicated to cooking for one.

Crafting, DIY, or Gardening Party for One

Want something tangible at the end of your solo time? I have a friend who spent hours on a design presentation for herself for a remodel of her own home. She loved to research and try all different building and décor options. Just because it's PowerPoint doesn't mean it's all work and no play. Hit up YouTube for inspirational videos and take time to learn all about your craft or project.

Spreadsheets of Joy

Lots of people keep PowerPoints or lists or spreadsheets of fun things: all the concerts they've been to, all the books they've read, movies they want to see, vacations they want to go on. One of my spreadsheets of joy is all restaurants—often with specific dishes to order—I want to visit on my next trip to New Orleans!

Theme Nights

Watch HGTV and start a new Pinterest board with the ideas you get. Page through *1000 Places to See Before You Die* and go around the internet and price out your top three favorites. Could you afford to see Bali in the spring?

Chore Night Party for One

The house needs to be cleaned, along with laundry, mail sorting, and the like. Sure! Chores can be a party for one. Everyone has to do the drudgery, but as the head of your household, you can do them whenever you want. Maybe you are grumbling that if you had a partner, you would have half the housework or errands. Google "couples chore wars" and remind yourself that living alone, *you* set the cleanliness level and the chore schedule, which is a blessing. Blast any music you want. Give yourself a power hour of chores, then have a reward waiting for yourself. I have one friend who believes in always lighting scented candles as she cleans. Sounds like a lovely ritual to me, and I've adopted it as part of my cleaning process!

Cleaning as a party? It's a stretch, but looking forward to your time alone is not. Making the most of the activities—exciting or mundane—you do in your solo time is a valuable skill to cultivate for the rest of your life. Take ownership that you are spending time as you choose to make yourself happy.

When it comes to your time in your own company, what would feel good? It's a party for one and you are the only guest you have to make happy. All day, every day.

Chapter Nineteen

Party of One: Going Out Solo

Date yourself! Oh, that old bit of cheerful advice seems simplistic and sad. Take a thing made for couples like dating and do it...alone. That seems, well, very much...not fun.

However, if you want to make the best of your solo time, you *will* want to get out and about by yourself. It's worth it to make the effort to be sure that even though you may not have a partner, or your friends are busy, you still get to go out and do things you like solo. Why should you miss out on enjoyable outings because you are solo? And, maybe, some events are more fun attended alone.

Consider the amount of time you would spend thinking about a date you were excited about. Now put some of that energy into time out with yourself. You are going to be with yourself for the rest of your life, so you should know how to treat yourself right!

Here are a few practical things to make yourself comfortable for a solo outing:

- Be sure to think ahead and really contemplate your own comfort. Wear something you feel comfortable and confident in. Perhaps you want to blend in and just wear jeans and a T-shirt or the urban all-black uniform. Maybe you like to make a statement when you walk in a room, so feeling good to you means a red sweater and eye-catching jewelry. Whatever it is, be sure you feel comfortable and confident. Solo adventures are not the time for cumbersome purses or outerwear or not quite comfortable shoes.

- Scope out the physical setup. Preview where you are going online first. Does the physical setting look good to you? Can you see yourself there? Or do they have dining-friendly seats at the bar if you feel like a more atmospheric experience? Are there places you can sit with your back to a wall so you can see the crowd? Are the seats far enough away from other folks that you won't feel like you are eavesdropping?

•Know how you are getting home. If you are going to have some drinks, will it be easy to get an Uber or cab? Will there be a long valet or parking line that will be an end of night buzzkill?

•Have backup entertainment on your person. Carry the newspaper or grab a local tourism magazine. Get your phone out and read or play a game. You can amuse yourself. Watch the ball game in a bar. Enjoy some people watching.

•Know that if it isn't fun, you can leave. You are making the effort to make yourself happy, and if you aren't happy, just move on.

•Think about if you want to engage with other people. I am an introverted extrovert, so I enjoy the time to myself in my own company. Other people like to chat up their neighbors at an event to share the experience. Be clear on which one you are as you pick your setting or event. Also think about who you might want to chat up to ease any social anxiety. Bartenders or servers are working for gratuity. They are great resources to say, "I'm here solo and want to be comfortable."

•Focus on the actual activity, not your solo status. Pick something you are excited about doing or seeing or experiencing. If you love the music at a concert or are looking forward to the food at a restaurant, you will have less focus on being solo. If you are participating in an activity that takes up your energy, that's good.

I know going out to an event alone can be daunting, and I have had good and bad experiences going out solo. I am a foodie. I love to taste and try and research restaurants. See how chefs work and how food is presented. Chicago hosts Chicago Gourmet, a very swanky outdoor food festival. It's an upscale see-and-be-seen crowd and I have mostly attended solo. I really come to see the vendors. I can freely move through the crowd and nosh and taste as I wish — no negotiating with a group. No asking, "What do *you* want to do next?" I actually have more fun going solo.

At a different foodie event, I had less of a positive experience. I went to a chef's dinner at an oceanside restaurant in Miami maybe an hour's drive from where I live. I was so excited! I made a day of it and booked a room nearby so I wouldn't have to drive home. It was inside a small and beautiful dining room with a very upscale crowd. Somehow the assigned seating wasn't correct. Since I was by myself and the tables all had even number seats, it took a few very long minutes to find a spot for me. As an experienced event person, I understood the challenge and I was able to keep myself fairly calm as I stood solo and displaced among seated diners. The best solution the restaurant came up with was to seat me as the seventh guest at the end of a six-top with three couples. Oomph. Ugh. The group of six all knew each other very well and their children all went to school together. They were not inclusive of me, to say the least. One of the women even said my name was "too complicated to remember" *as I introduced myself* and they carried on an animated conversation...excluding me throughout the evening.

It was awful. I focused on the beauty of the room

and the delicious food. I was polite, but after a few attempts, I stopped trying to make conversation with the group. Early on, I went to where the servers were gathered to bring plates out and I said, "I've been assigned to this table and they are being not so friendly; please don't let my wine glass run dry!" With that plea, along with how obvious it was that I was being excluded, the waitstaff didn't let me down. I had offers for water and wine and bread and seconds every few minutes throughout dinner! It's a funny story, but it certainly was hurtful at the time. I just kept reminding myself that it was only a few hours of my life and my table partners were being oblivious and dumb, rather than unkind or actually attacking me in any way.

Another big event I went to solo was a black-tie Mardi Gras party in New Orleans. I was so excited to get a VIP ticket but intimidated to go alone. Even the guy who gave me the ticket questioned why I wanted to be there solo. But even though I was nervous, I still thought I could enjoy myself. It was a 20,000-attendee event in the NOLA convention center with amazing décor and endless food and bar and terrific entertainment and costumes and gussied up guests (aka, *amazing*). I wore a great dress. I had to stand solo in a long line to get into the party, but I had read online that was part of the entry process, so I was able to fight off the "everyone is here with someone" feelings.

The party itself did not disappoint! I scoped out the physical setup and walked all around the party to see where I might feel most comfortable. I ended up behind the concert sound engineer near the entrance to the VIP section—I was a little bit hidden but could see all the people come and go. The Mardi Gras parades entered the party and threw beads into the crowd. I was sharing what I caught with these two older ladies who were sisters. They had been to this big fancy party a million times and we shared a few laughs. Just that little bit of interaction made me super comfortable. I was really impressed with this soiree I was attending for the first time, but they were regulars and shared a "join in the fun" attitude. Those were the only people I talked to and stayed until 3 a.m. enjoying the bands and the people watching and the vibe. All by myself.

One last story from my Party of One adventures. I

was in Las Vegas for work with a free night and I went to see a sexy cirque de something show. I was sitting alone in the theater in the round. Within ten minutes, two sets of newlyweds asked me to take their cute couple photo, which I did. I'm always game to snap a pic of folks, but, yes, I felt it — singled out — my solo status. It was a weeknight, so the theater was practically empty. An usher had watched me come in alone and get hit up twice to be the couples' unofficial house photographer. He got my attention and without a word moved me to my own solo box with a better view and complimentary champagne. You know how they say the world loves a lover? I kinda think the world has a soft spot for cool ladies rolling solo too.

Now hopefully you are inspired and ready to take yourself out into the world. Where do you want to go? Sure, it's easy to stay home, but if you pick outings you love, it's much more fun!

Think of all the places you already go alone: the grocery store, the gym, outdoor walks, the library, the airport, etc. Are more social environments really *that* different if you think about it? I go to a carwash where you have to hang out for, like, twenty minutes while you wait for them to call you to get your car. It reminds me of a social setting where no one knows each other. I always think this would be a great place to practice going to a social setting solo. So next time you are out alone doing errands, remind yourself that you can be just as comfortable solo in a social setting too.

If you are still building your skill set of getting out in the world solo, here are few scenarios to get your started:

Movies

This is a basic. If you have never gone to the movies alone, you should just do it as a rite of passage. No one is paying attention to who else is at the movies. Maybe skip the opening of the summer blockbuster on a Friday night in June when every tween will be there, but if you want to see a movie, go and enjoy. No sidekick needed. You can eat whatever treat you want, sit wherever you want, and pick your own timing. Skip or savor the previews as you wish. Once the lights go down, it's really just an audience of one anyway. This is a great starter solo excursion

Museums or Tours

There isn't supposed to be talking and interacting at these types of cultural events, so go, absorb, and get cultured.

Drinks or Dinner

You don't have to go to the romantic steakhouse on February 13. Go out for brunch or breakfast and read the paper. Have lunch late when the crowds are thinner. Go for an early dinner. Sit at the bar. Going to a restaurant solo can very enjoyable.

I moved to a beach town where going out to dinner is a big activity and many folks are single or retired. I was renovating a condo and there was not much space for dining in my home, so every few days I would treat myself to a nice foodie outing. Every time I sat down at a bar and ordered a glass of wine, the bartender would extend themselves. Always told me their name and shook my hand if I offered. I thought it was noticeable that the bartenders had my back by being especially personal and welcoming. Yes, I did text my friends and play Scrabble on my phone. But I also soaked up the atmosphere and enjoyed myself.

Another trick to enjoying drinks or dining out alone is to be a regular. Go to the same restaurant at the same time each week. I learned this trick when I would travel to work an event and stay in a different city for weeks and weeks at a time. I would immediately start a routine of going to the same coffee place each morning or pick the same dinner place a few nights a week. It's entirely possible the vibe and the people will be the same, ensuring your comfort level with each visit.

Want know how long it takes to become a regular at a restaurant or coffee place? Three visits and a solid 20 percent gratuity policy coupled with a "Thanks, this was great" every time you visit. That's community and it's waiting for you.

Concerts

This scenario is like going to the movies. You attend

a concert for the stage performance and the collective excitement. My strategy with a solo concert is to wait until the day before or the day of the concert to commit. If you are going to a musical event, I feel like some emotion will play into it and you want to be in "the mood." I also like to buy an end seat or a seat with empty seats by it. It gives you a little space—elbow room and psychological—and, frankly, an escape route. I also try to buy the very best seat I can afford. I'd rather skip the beverages and upgrade the ticket. I think the crowd nearby is more invested and the show is closer and more enjoyable.

I once bought a last-minute ticket to Billy Joel at Wrigley Field and sat with the guy who sold me the solo ticket. He was supposed to attend with his wife and another couple and they all bailed on him at the last minute. I bought him a drink to thank him for selling one of his extras. He and I had a blast entirely based on our love of the Piano Man. If you are lost in the music, who you're with can be less important.

I hope these examples inspire you to do something fun by yourself. You can always leave if you aren't having fun. Put some thought into how to make yourself comfortable and what you might find the most pleasurable. Then give it a try.

Chapter Twenty

Party Beyond One: Going Out to Connect

Eventually you will want to go out in group settings that involve meeting others. The first type of event that comes to mind might be…a singles event! To meet a potential partner! A dating advice book will better help you strategize attending those kinds of events. My one piece of related advice is to pick a singles-only event that has a second common interest. Single as a marital status is not necessarily a commonality. It's best to have the second commonality or interest like a favorite sport or a love of travel or shared activity.

Being a part of different types of communities is one of the joys of singlehood and is excellent for your mental health and well-being. Here are a few helpful tips on your mindset for successful group activities:

1. When choosing an activity to join for meeting people, do something you would normally want to do no matter the crowd. If you love hiking and you meet a hiking group, you can talk about hiking and enjoy hiking. You already have a commonality at the start. Meetup is a website that allows people with similar interests to arrange events and "meet up" to enjoy their mutual interest together. There are sports leagues, fitness groups, book clubs, cultural outings, dog owner clubs, business interest groups, and countless other gatherings all over the country. Or look into activities at your local recreation center, library, alumni group, or chamber of commerce.

2. As long as you enjoy the activity, the fresh air or a change of your usual scenery — and maybe a nosh and some wine — will do you good. Who the heck cares who's there? Just be, blend in, and enjoy the activity at hand. With a little practice, this is a great mindset and confidence boost.

3. Everyone loves an optimist. You don't have to be outgoing, gregarious, or different from yourself,

but you do have to be positive and pleasant. Plain and simple—nod your head yes. I have a friend who attended Notre Dame and talked about going to the student Mass on Sunday nights as a study break even though he wasn't Catholic. I asked him why he went and he replied, "Everyone else was going." I am not saying be a lemming and blindly participate, but a little bit of "go along to get along" in social situations with new folks can do wonders. Downside: you might be bored. Upside: you have a happy experience you might not have expected.

4. We have more commonalities than you think. We all put pants on, pay taxes, think about the seasons, drive cars, and watch TV. Look for topics that connect, not divide.

5. Wherever two or more are gathered, it's entirely possible someone won't be your type (to paraphrase). When attending an activity, remember you chose to join in, so pack your patience and be kind to everyone involved. For best results, communicate your acceptance to others (verbally and non-verbally, please). Again,

seek to connect, not divide. It will lighten the mood and create acceptance of you in others.

6. The kindest and best soloist approach is to find something lovable about the people you meet in social circumstances. I don't care if someone has a small second head growing out of their forehead, as long as that person and their forehead head are displaying good intent, I am happy to be friendly.

7. Prepare yourself a bit for a best and worst outcome. If you are nervous, really think about it in advance. Think about getting to the parking lot and being nervous. What will you tell yourself? Imagine introducing yourself or handling registration. It's OK to be nervous, and those nerves are easier to manage when you expect to manage them in the moment.

8. Remind yourself no one is watching you. Remind yourself over and over again.

9. Remind yourself this is one outing for a limited time once in your life. Remind yourself over and over again. Coach yourself up.

10. Manage your expectations. Let's say you sign up for a tennis outing. Your expectations should be the following:

- I am going to play tennis.

- I will be in a tennis setting.

- Other people will be there.

- No more, no less.

Here's what *not* to think;

- I am totally going to mesh with this group and it will be so awesome. We will form a group of professional level tennis players and get jackets with our names embroidered on them. I can see all my new tennis friends gathered around my tennis racket shaped birthday cake next year!

- I will be the worst tennis player anyone has ever seen. They will all watch and point and laugh when I trip over my own serve while wearing the ugliest tennis outfit ever to walk the court.

•I am the world's greatest weekend tennis player, and these people will be so thankful that I have come into their group. I'll bet they will ask me to host a workshop on the rules of tennis for the next meeting.

11. Finally, leave if you don't like it.

•There's no reason to suffer.

•You don't owe anyone anything.

•Sometimes the vibe isn't right. Sometimes you just aren't in the mood.

•The event isn't what you expected. The upside of making solo plans is you can depart. No harm, no foul.

•Your party beyond one can immediately become a party of one back at home or the Starbucks on the next block.

Maybe it takes you a few tries to follow through and show up to a group event. That's OK. Even if you go to an event and leave, you learned *something* about what you like about going to an event. You have to try out different group outings so you can find a good fit. Some trial and error is to be expected.

Attracting Another Party of One While Going Out to Connect

If you go out in the world, someone might find you attractive.

If anyone communicates that they are romantically attracted to you, it is a compliment of the highest order.

But what if the attention is from someone you think is not so great or not so appropriate or not so polite? Mostly, there's no need to sound the alarm. Don't think about it too long or too hard — just take it at face value. In my thirties, I lived in Florida and would get hit on by guys well into their seventies and I would be furious. Do I look that old? Who does he think he is? *Who cares?* Just communicate a firm and sweet "No, thank you" and move on.

It takes courage to reveal one's feelings to another human being, and it is unacceptable for the recipient to be anything but gracious and kind. No matter the kind of package or the type of approach, if you are not interested, a simple and direct "Thanks for saying hi; will you please excuse me," or "Nice to meet you; I was just headed to the door/to my friend/to check my phone" is all it takes to say no. Attraction and meeting people is tricky and people can be dumb.

Be gentle with the opposite sex as you would want someone to be kind with you.

Of course, if you feel physically threatened or fearful, get a third party involved, remove yourself from the situation, and put your own safety first.

Chapter Twenty-One

The Future: Don't Wait

It can sometimes feel like finding and committing to a partner is finally adulthood. Or that *not* having a partner makes you a second-class citizen. You may feel like you don't quite have the right or the resources to do life's "big stuff" by yourself. Oh, but you do!

Your life has started. It's here. It's happening. You do not need anyone's permission to do big things with your life and your future. Even if it's "just" you, enjoy anything you wish.

Allow yourself to feel empowered. There is not one reason why you cannot achieve any goal or enjoy any reward in this life all by yourself. If you really want something, create it for yourself. Never deny yourself anything while waiting for a partner.

As you think about creating your future from exactly where your life is today, remember you only live once. Tomorrow is promised to none of us, so making the most of *every* stage of life is so important.

Social Life

Believe in your own grown-up status as a family of one. Just because you're not partnered doesn't mean you are a half citizen in your own social life. You are a family of one. You don't come last or as a token add-on. Your plans and wants are not secondary because it's "just me." Elevate your social status in your own head and those in your life who love you will follow.

Buy the House or Condo

You can always sell it. You can handle the responsibility and it's a massive upside financially. I had a friend who was sassy, professional, and money wise. She owned a minivan and a three-bedroom house. She was single and thirty-six and drove her minivan to work every day. "I thought if I bought it, they would come," she said. "They" being the husband and children she longed for. Why would you shortchange yourself like that? Buy what works for your life right now. Living life with the Ghosts of Imagined Family Future is not a happy existence, and, practically speaking, you do not know what your future partner or family life will look like, so it is not a good use of energy.

Hang the Art on the Walls

When you move in somewhere, make it your home for whatever amount of time you will be there. Do not think, *I'll wait until someone comes along to really have a home. This is just for me. I'll get carpet, nice dishes, and maybe a lawnmower when I get married.* Do not think, *It's just me, I don't need any upgrades.* Your home for your family of one should be exactly what fits you right now. Embracing it doesn't determine the future. But it sure makes the present much more enjoyable and livable.

Parenting

There are all kinds of ways to have children in your

life. If you have time in your life and space in your heart, volunteer or get involved in a routine way with the children already in your life. If being a mother calls out to your soul, and you know you must have a little person in your life, you can do it. Do more than wish about it. There is a tremendous amount of internet information about this very question. What is the process? How would you do it? What would it look like? Researching an active, doable solo solution is whole lot better than being sad when baby shower invites arrive in your inbox.

Before noon on my thirty-eighth birthday, three older women in my life who I really respect, separately said to me some version of, "You have to have a baby this year." I was dumbfounded. Had I reached some milestone? I was not in a relationship. I was traveling 120 days a year doing a job I loved. Their advice was given in love and I heard it. After one weeping phone call to one of my favorite mothers of five children pals, I took a deep breath, then considered my options. I talked and prayed about it. I very seriously considered what having a family on my own could look like. The answer *for me* has been to be a terrific aunt. Five years later, I needed to have a hysterectomy, and I had already done the work to know for sure how I felt about not having children of my own. Exploring your options can bring the peace of making a good decision for yourself.

Jewelry

You have nine other fingers besides your left-hand wedding ring finger. You also have a neck, wrists, and ears. If you have 1200 photos of wedding ring sets saved on Pinterest and you have the money, get yourself some bling already!

Travel

So, you think Virginia is only for lovers? Virginia's most popular tourist site is Colonial Williamsburg, so that is just a state marketing campaign!

How could you see the canals of Venice without someone's hand to hold in the Piazza? So many people get married in Hawaii—how could you go solo? Just go already. Talk to the widow who put off the trip or the partner who has a spouse who doesn't like adventures. Better yet, talk to someone who went somewhere solo and had a blast!

Think about Venice. There is the classic image of a lovey-dovey couple tucked into a gondola at sunset kissing and floating to the romantic strings of Italian music. Fun. Another fantasy is being single, visiting Italy, and being invited to meet the handsome gondolier on the canal bridge at midnight for a prosecco and gondola ride and some kissing of your own! The only chance of meeting the gondola driver (or eating the pasta or riding in the gondola) is if you actually get on an airplane and visit Italy. Consolation prize if you don't fall in love with an Italian? A trip to Italy! That's a win-win.

Yes, I had that keepsake adventure with a sexy gondolier! The only actual communication we accomplished in words was he was worried about my *bianco* sweater getting dirty. I was like, "It's from TJ Maxx, let's keep making out in this gondola."

The Party—A Special Note on Weddings

Weddings certainly result in quite a few gatherings, don't they? Bridal shower, engagement party, engagement photo reveal party, bachelorette party, rehearsal dinner, wedding, next day brunch. Add in the welcome baby and anniversary events and it can sometimes feel like the singleton never gets a big bash.

At one point, I moved to a new city, bought and set up a new home, started a business, graduated from college then graduate school, yet it felt like no one had so much as bought me a cupcake, let alone celebrated with a glass clinking followed by teary-eyed toasts. I definitely thought, *Where's* my *shower?*

So, guess what? I threw my own party. I celebrated a big birthday and the invitation literally announced a contest for who could bring me the best gift! (Read *The 5 Love Languages* books—gifts are one of my love languages.) If you have people in your life, then you can certainly give yourself a party.

Can't afford a big shindig to compete with all those weddings you are attending? Throw yourself a brunch, a wiener roast, a housewarming, or a Christmas tree decorating party. Think of it as a way to celebrate your friendships. Show your loved ones how much you care about them *and* let them show they care about you.

The wedding business is a $6 billion a year industry. Marketing is a huge factor in wedding lust. Challenge yourself to examine those wedding feelings. Is it the photos? Pay to have your portrait taken by a pro and use them to represent you online. Is it the dress? Go on a cruise or attend or volunteer at a black-tie event and get your fancy dress on! Is it having "your day"? Your day is every day.

Take care of yourself very well and build a solo so full that a wedding will be just one happy day in your life of many happy days.

Chapter Twenty-Two

Money: It's All Yours

Do you want to forego expensive goods and give to charity?

Do you want to have a nice car or an expensive handbag?

What's the best way for you to give those things to yourself?

Do you want to recover from a financially harmful divorce?

Do you want to give your children a positive financial role model?

Do you want to spend your money on experiences?

How much money in the bank makes you feel secure?

Striving for the best single life demands that you examine how it's going to be funded. Financial decisions can be overwhelming. Having a partner with an additional skill set and approach (and income stream) to strategize a financial plan can be an advantage.

But when you are sharing a financial life with someone, there's someone to cheat on or monitor you, depending on if you are the saver or the spender in the relationship. Having a partner can be detrimental to your financial status if they act in a reckless or selfish way.

When you are single, it's all up to you, so you can control the outcome. The results of investments, savings, and sound financial decisions are enjoyed by you. How you manage your money is a tangible category for you to live your values.

Often, a partnership or marriage forces a person into making adult money decisions. Do not wait for that milestone; you should make informed money decisions as soon as possible. After a divorce, financial plans need to be reassessed for a single person. This is a positive thing. No matter where you are starting financially, you alone can get yourself to a better financial position by understanding your finances and setting yourself up for success.

Be Your Own Advocate and Become (or Consult) an Expert

There are so many resources online and professionals ready to assist you in understanding your finances and creating and meeting money goals. Make a commitment to yourself to learn everything you need to be comfortable with your finances. Become your own best expert.

Plan Financially for Your Life as It Is Today

Base your finances on your life right now. Don't buy a big house because it will be great for a husband and kids when currently neither exist in your life. Don't spend recklessly, betting that a partner will come along with money to take care of you in your old age. Hold yourself accountable to learn about finances now as a Family of One.

Save

Stash some cash for a rainy day or a year's downpour. Have enough money that you have options, as life, health, family, and career changes happen. More money means more choices.

Set Financial Goals

As a single person, life can sometimes feel uncertain, with an undercurrent of *what if I meet someone?* Or you are transitioning from being in a partnership to a new single life. These adjustments are not factors in your financial life. You are responsible for you financially, with or without a partner.

Understand Your Money

You only need a paper and pen and the ability to face your financial truth. What are your monthly bills? How much do you earn? How do you file and pay for your taxes? How much debt do you have? How much debt are you comfortable carrying? What kind of income and expenditures are you planning for the next month or six months or five years?

If you know clearly where you stand, you can plan for where you want to be.

Chapter Twenty-Three

Side Hustles

Without the time demands of a partner, you might have some free time in your life. If you want to bridge the gap between doing your best to be responsible for yourself financially and filling your time with activities you love, may I introduce the side hustle. This is a part-time job in addition to your main job and often includes a fun element. Look at what you enjoy doing, then be imaginative and see if there is a way to find limited time or temporary employment doing something you love. You can also find a side hustle that meets some of your social needs.

After college, I moved to Chicago. I had an office job during the week and not a lot of extra cash, so I got a waitressing job. It was at a casual bar in a swanky neighborhood that served breakfast. I would bike to work (no need for a gym membership!). I worked on Saturday and Sunday mornings, so the bar, which might have been a bit dingy and busy at night, was bright and not too crowded for the weekend breakfast shift. I got to know the neighborhood, made friends with the regulars, ate heartily, and made cash! I still could socialize on a Saturday night and if I timed it right, I could use the tip money I made to get an indulgent manicure and pay for my weekend fun!

In my thirties, I was keenly aware of being single and dreamed of hosting the big family holidays. I wanted to be the "lady of the house," and for me that meant being in charge of the family table. I loved to cook. I loved to organize a kitchen, use beautiful kitchenware, and even scrub that kitchen back to sparkling clean. So, I became a caterer.

It became my side hustle.

I poured over cookbooks, obsessively watched the Food Network, and researched tips and tricks online. I got the courage to spread the word of my side hustle among friends. I did some practice gigs for people I knew (who, in hindsight, were very patient with my learning curve). Next, I put an ad on Craigslist offering my services. I started small and limited my scope to private parties in private homes. Word spread. I loved it and did it for years. With my family scattered, I wasn't much of a holiday person, so I worked Christmas and New Year's Eve for other wonderful families. Sometimes I cooked and sometimes I just served, but I made terrific money doing something I love. I got to be that "lady of the house" and create beautiful holiday dinners in beautiful kitchens — no husband and no mortgage needed.

When Uber first started, I took one to the deep suburbs of the Midwest. My driver was a single mom who said the minute her ex picked up her children, she got in the car and started driving. She made money, met new people, talked to adults, visited places in her city she had never seen before, and got out of her too quiet house. She could pick her own hours based on her children's needs and changing schedules.

Before you think about a specific job, think about your passion. What activities are fun? A side hustle can be fun and social, plus bring in a little cash. Do you dream of changing careers but need to continue at the job you have to pay the bills? Well, you can side hustle small parts in all kinds of industries. Want to be an actress? Be an extra or an usher in the theater. Visions of authoring a best seller? Write a blog or tutor kids in writing. Interior designer or real estate ambition? Offer to work hourly doing small tasks to learn the business from someone you admire.

Are you athletic? Maybe your local running shoe store or paddle boarding provider could use an extra person on busy weekends or during their special event offerings. All kinds of gyms and workout offerings need teachers.

Challenge yourself.

Do you like to cook? You don't have to start a solo in-home service like I did. Caterers, specialty chefs, or cooking classes hire staff to do some of the endless kitchen work in serving meals to lots of folks or keeping a classroom full of amateur cooks in clean counter space.

When you became single, did you downsize? If you

have the money, you could buy a nearby property and do Airbnb. Or are you an empty nester and have a room to rent?

Do you love gaming? Or internet research? Learn to code and create and sell an app.

Do you love to create art? Get yourself to Etsy right now. You can start small and bring beauty to your customers.

Are you a caretaker? Tutor or nanny or walk dogs or clean houses or do tutorials on YouTube. Are you a shopper? Then pick up a few shifts at the mall or a sole proprietor owned shop. You never know what kind of work schedule you can get until you ask!

If any from the list above struck you at all, you owe it to yourself to investigate. What kind of time can you give a side hustle? See what's out there. Maybe you don't need to make a commitment. Start small or just the holidays or just the summer. Your mindset is your choice, and you never know what kind of wonderful situation you can find until you ask around.

If money isn't a motivator for you, side hustle

rewards are very similar to volunteer opportunities. Start investigating where you can donate your best resource — your time!

Knowing yourself well enough to know what to avoid in a side hustle is as important as being drawn to your passions when it comes to spending time on a side hustle.

Chapter Twenty-Four

The End of Life

"Till death do us part" is not just for marriage vows. It applies to everyone. Just as your solo will not last forever, neither will your life here on earth. No one likes to think of an untimely end, but you are an adult and the head of your family of one. You have a responsibility to make your wishes known to your loved ones. While facing your own demise is difficult, it is a very loving thing to do for your family and friends. If you die without a spouse or a will, you are creating a significant—emotional, financial, and logistical—burden on your parents, siblings, children, and/or friends.

I dated a very recently divorced chiropractor and he mentioned he had changed his will. He said, "I took back my retirement for myself but I gave my ex the house. If something were to happen to me, she would have a big responsibility to raise our children. But I hope that in five years she and I will both have progressed. She is more established, and I hope to have a new partner. I'll update my will again and include that person." It is strong and practical to acknowledge the different stages post-divorce. As you age through your solo, your feelings and circumstances are sure to evolve, therefore, regularly reviewing your end-of-life wishes is an essential practice.

Get a Will

If you are an adult, you have stuff. Who is going to get it? Intestate is dying without a will. If that happens, the next step is the probate court process, which may take six to eighteen months. With a few hours of your time and a downloaded form from the internet, you can avoid that for your family and be clear with how you want to share your resources if something were to happen to you.

Celebration of Life

Pick a quiet time and set a time limit—less than an hour even. Send an email to a trusted friend or family member, "I hope you never need this" in the subject line. Just put something in writing of how you would want your life celebrated. Name a church or gathering place and mention if you want a party. Think of a playlist or a menu if that inspires you. Maybe start with what you don't want (e.g., no wearing black, poetry not the Bible, etc.). Keep it simple. Even a few bullet points would be so valuable if they were needed.

Shut It Down

While grieving their child, do you want your parents to have to call your bank and tell them you don't need your credit card anymore? At the very least, ask a specific loved one to handle your finances. Tell that person where your password list and important paperwork are. At the other extreme, I asked in my will that a specific friend be present if my home needed to be cleared of my belongings. I picked someone emotionally capable who knows my values and my circle of friends and family so that my home and belongings would be treated with discretion and distributed in a way that would be consistent with my values.

Friends Meet Friends

In a single lifestyle, it's easy to have work friends, church friends, family friends, and college friends each in separate worlds. Those folks may know about each other, but do they know each other's last names? Do they have each other's cell phone numbers? Do you know the last name of the man your friend from your hometown moved in with? You just might not. Introduce your inner circle to one another. I put close friends on texts together every now and again. I've introduced my sister to my financial planner. The people who love you from different parts of your life have the same goal: to support you. Why not mix the groups? Hint: if you bring all the people you like and who like you together, they are probably going to like each other!

Full disclosure: I picked the brother (who happens to be a lawyer) of a good friend of mine. He's someone who has been in my social circle for more than twenty years. I know his values and he knows mine. I trust him to be practical and kind. We've had two discussions about this end-of-life topic in ten years. Both included martinis at swanky bars and a lot of humor.

It's likely your end-of-life wishes will change, so commit to doing a review every five years. Then take care of yourself the best you can so that the paperwork is never needed!

Chapter Twenty-Five

Live Well and Have Standards

No matter your partner status, no one is standing in line to take care of you in this life. That's up to you, so as you build your solo, think about what your standards are.

When in a relationship, you might be motivated by the presence of a partner to keep the kitchen clean every night before bed. Or you think, *My partner is coming over; I want to be sure I look nice and should make the bed.* Or you and your partner make an agreement to have and encourage each other's healthy exercise and nutrition habits. Meanwhile, it can be easy to just slide into life on your own. It takes effort, motivation, and thought to set and maintain standards for yourself. You must decide you are worth it. You will benefit.

When you are newly dating someone, you plan a

whole weekend together and in your mind's eye you see every detail. The food, the setting, the conversation, your outfit. Bring that same energy to your whole life. If a potential partner is worth that effort, then you are worth that effort and more!

First, you need consider your values so you can use your limited time and resources on areas you consider important as you build your solo life. Here are a few categories of questions about lifestyle. Note what inspires you.

Appearance

Just because you are solo does not mean you can let your personal hygiene or appearance slide. Keep up with haircuts and skincare. Do you want to spend time and money to be a fashionista, or do you want to be like Obama and Zuckerberg, saving yourself from making a daily clothing decision by wearing the same "uniform" most days? You don't need to be taller or thinner or younger, but looking good will help you feel good. What does looking good look like to you? You don't have to be a supermodel, but clean yoga pants every day is a worthy goal. Shaving and bikini waxes — only when you have a sex partner or all the time?

Wellness and Health

What's your exercise plan? What kind of exercise do you like? Are some physical activities daily and others weekly? Will you keep track of health screenings without someone hounding you? It's easy to say, "I'll quit smoking when I meet someone," or, "There's no one here, so why not finish this bag of chips in one day." How will you measure your mental, emotional, and spiritual wellness?

Appearance of Your Home

Your home is your sanctuary. Your private refuge. Maybe you had a big house and busy life with a partner and when you think of your solo life, you want minimalism. Maybe you are setting up your first household without a partner and you relish personal choices like furniture and lighting. Maybe you want to spend your money and energy on experiences outside your home, so you keep it very simple. Are you going to put up holiday decorations? How much time do you want to spend on upkeep?

Meals

I am a foodie. Dining is important to me. I cook for myself. I use cloth napkins even when dining alone. I saw a movie on TV and a cowboy type character said, "I don't care what I eat." Which one are you? Maybe you want a lot of specialty vinegars to whip up your own salad dressing for each salad you eat or maybe you prefer the same sandwich for lunch every day. Maybe you want to budget in your favorite takeout and balance that with at home meals. Feeding yourself is important for a healthy body and mind. How do you want to do it?

Social Interaction

Use it or lose it. Can you picture the cranky old man neighbor shouting, "Get off my lawn!"? I empathize with him! Those neighbor kids probably surprised him and his solitary day, so he barked at them! But that's not an excuse. If you live with others, you get regular feedback on using a nice tone. But it's easy to forget if you live alone. How will you remind yourself to stay friendly to others?

Think about your neighbors. Maybe you want to set a standard that you always stop to greet them. Or maybe you want to be more private and just wave and keep it moving. I was leading a group of singles on vacation, and when I got up to use the restroom, one woman barked at me, "Where are you going?!" I thought, *Why is she yelling at me?* Then I realized from the little I knew about her, she was an adult single living with her parents in a still adolescent family set up. Without a partner or an active social life, she was out of practice on familiar but polite interactions.

Schedule

Do you just let your days, weeks, and months of leisure time drift by? Or do you manage and plan your alone time as a Family of One just like you would if you were a family of multiple people? Good weekends are built from fun and chores and rest and projects and errands. What does that look like to you? Do you want to tackle exercise and chores and social obligations on Saturdays so you can be lazy all-day Sunday? Make that commitment with yourself.

Function

Does your life and household function? How would you change how you live if a friend you admired came to live with you next week? Is your ex's stuff still at your house? Do you have an attic that looks like six people live at your house and it's just you? A few boxes of decorations for the holidays is great, but is holding onto other stuff holding you back? Does everything in your house work? A friend went to the laundromat instead of getting her washer fixed because it was "just my stuff." That is not making your life work for you.

These questions should help you understand your standards and how you want to be in the world. Committing to standards in the categories you care about will give you confidence and pleasure. The better your life feels from the inside, the better you will feel. People will react more positively to you, and you will better be able to handle life's ups and downs. The more you own your choices of how you spend your time and effort, the less room there is for resentment or feeling like you are missing something. Choose how you want your life to feel, then live those choices.

Final Note

It takes thoughtful effort and good choices to build a solo you love. I hope you have found lots of inspiration here on seeing the solo stage of life more clearly and these insights will inspire you to act in your life. Be kind and generous with yourself. Be aware of your thoughts and feelings about being solo. Take advantage of this time to truly know yourself and what makes you happy. The better you know yourself and the happier your solo life, the more capable you are to have better relationships with others. You are also more ready to build the kind of social life you desire and have a diverse and robust friend group.

In your solo, you are a complete and valid Family of One. Remember, romantic love within a relationship is not the only game in town. I promise you love and validation are all around. Life is waiting for you to take the stage and begin your solo.

Call to Action

Putting a positive message into the world about singlehood has been a goal of MY solo. I am thrilled you picked up this book and I invite you to continue the conversation!

You can send thoughts or questions directly to me at enjoyyoursolobook@gmail.com.

You are welcome to join the conversation on social media on Instagram @enjoyyoursolo and on Facebook at the Enjoy Your Solo Facebook Group

You can join the EYS community by signing up for a newsletter at www.themarydelia.com.

You can spread the word in social media by using #EYS or #EnjoyYourSolo next time you are enjoying your best solo life! Selfies welcome!

You can support my one-woman self-publishing

journey by leaving a review at Amazon.com. A simple review is a huge boost!!

Thank you for allowing me to be part of YOUR solo!

Mary Delia

Acknowledgements

Thank you to all who encouraged and supported me. Evidence of my successful solo has been shown to me by the sheer volume and pure, genuine reactions I have received from the people in my life while bringing this book into the world.

Special thanks to:

Cara for always believing in me (and this book!).

Kelly for being the original and kindest idiot mirror.

Peggy, the best sister for a never-ending game of Lady Friend, many elements of which echo an enjoyable solo!

For all the singles:

My heart is in these pages to help you build your very best solo, so I truly hope you ENJOY!

Printed in Great Britain
by Amazon

15231438R00119